International Acclaim for *In the L*

"Few [political reporters] lay bare the ⟨...⟩ war-ravaged landscapes, but of the observer's soul. Daniel Bergner's book belongs in this tiny platoon. In the finest Orwellian tradition, it will discomfit readers across the political spectrum. . . . A drily ferocious, take-no-hostages style [and] crisply drawn characters . . . The best political writers may prepare us to shed our illusions. As Daniel Bergner proves, they don't demand that we abandon hope."

BOYD TONKIN, *The Independent* (U.K.)

"Fascinating and profoundly unsettling . . . Bergner is not only a vivid writer, but a great narrator. . . . Harrowing yet deeply moving . . . it is charged with echoes of our own daily lives. . . . One of the best books I've read in years."

—RON BUTLIN, *The Sunday Herald* (Scotland)

"An eloquent witness . . . The black and the white of Bergner's [subtitle] are, on the one hand, the victims of the seemingly endless civil war in Sierra Leone and, on the other, the missionaries, aid workers, and British soldiers who arrive to restore hope. Bergner follows such bleak narratives as that of Lamin, a husband and father whose hands were chopped off by the rebels, and Komba, a child soldier who calmly describes eating a victim's heart. . . . He [has] a journalist's eye for the telling moment; in one scene, amputees, coming to the polls to vote, pose happily for the cameras, while a member of the CNN crew says casually that the segment probably won't air in America."

—*The New Yorker*

"An intense, evocative depiction of the appalling conflict that tore Sierra Leone apart . . . Their tales are told with absorbing verve and pace and offer a glimpse into a heart of darkness that most of the world has chosen to ignore."

—ALBERT SMITH, *Irish Independent*

"Unusually candid . . . Bergner is a talented freelance writer who has artfully captured the horror and the anarchy of the civil war that ravaged Sierra Leone [and] provides a sharp contrast to the current situation in Iraq."

—Foreign Affairs magazine

"[Bergner] missed the bang-bang. But he offers something far more valuable: sharply drawn profiles that ultimately foretell the limits of the ongoing U.N. rescue mission. . . . Sierra Leone may be out of the news, but that makes its story all the more important."

—TOM MASLAND, Newsweek

"A searing, gruesome, and moving exploration of civil war at its worst. In the Land of Magic Soldiers presents the human faces of a conflict fought without humanity."

—Big Issue

"Mr. Bergner's book is a good one, in that he does not give way to caricatures. Even the killers are human, Janus-faced, and tragic."

—K. A. DILDAY, The New York Sun

"Daniel Bergner's stories of Sierra Leone's killers, victims, and rescuers are too intimate and beautifully told to be put aside. We're seldom lucky enough to get so talented a writer to make so sustained a commitment to so difficult and neglected a subject. Bergner has created humane literature about a war of cruelty beyond belief."

—GEORGE PACKER, author of Blood of the Liberals

"The journalist and novelist Daniel Bergner is right . . . to see Africa's civil wars as a horror of our time that deserves exploration. . . . A reminder of the potential [for killing and healing] that we all carry within us, of how precarious is the balance between them, and of how easily it can be tipped one way or the other by the societies we build for ourselves. In the Land of Magic Soldiers does not analyze the causes of Sierra Leone's war, but it reminds us of this precarious balance, and that may be the greater service."

—ADAM HOCHSCHILD, The New York Times Book Review

IN THE LAND OF MAGIC SOLDIERS

A STORY OF WHITE AND BLACK IN WEST AFRICA

DANIEL BERGNER

PICADOR

FARRAR, STRAUS AND GIROUX ■ **NEW YORK**

www.picadorusa.com

Picador® is a U.S. registered trademark and is used by Farrar, Straus and Giroux under license from Pan Books Limited.

For information on Picador Reading Group Guides, as well as ordering, please contact the Trade Marketing department at St. Martin's Press.
Phone: 1-800-221-7945 extension 763
Fax: 212-677-7456
E-mail: trademarketing@stmartins.com

Designed by Gretchen Achilles

Library of Congress Cataloging-in-Publication Data

Bergner, Daniel.
  In the land of magic soldiers : a story of white and black in West Africa / Daniel Bergner.
    p. cm.
  ISBN 0-312-42292-X
  EAN 978-0312-42292-9
  1. Sierra Leone—History—Civil War, 1991– I. Title.

DT516.826.B47 2003
966.404—dc21

2003044065

First published in the United States by Farrar, Straus and Giroux

First Picador Edition: October 2004

10 9 8 7 6 5 4 3 2 1

FOR NANCY

IN THE LAND OF MAGIC SOLDIERS

ONE There is a place where the bend in a path—just that, a slight curve in a narrow strip of mud—can produce an ache, a longing, a bending of the heart. Within the jungle on either side stand the cotton trees. Twelve stories high, their monstrous trunks fan out toward the earth in giant buttresses, forming the walls of strange rooms. To step inside those chambers, to have the massive growths enclose you, to lean with your feet on the spongy ground and your back to the cool damp bark, with almost all the sounds of the world absorbed by the misty air and the immensity of wood, is to exist in some other atmosphere, some softer medium, some fluid capable of sustaining you between this world and another.

And maybe it is only the nearness of those magical trees that causes the longing on the path. Or maybe it is the way the rainy-season light, filtering through the haze between storms, flickers off the undergrowth at the path's edge, making the leaves flash dimly like coins dropped into water, bright objects of little value sinking painfully out of reach. Or maybe it is the sheer thickness of all that greenery, the entire earth a depthless pillow to fall into. But I think it is also, up ahead, the minimal bend itself, leading the path so suddenly out of sight amidst the lush terrain, that puts a crimp in the chest, as though the heart has tried to close around something—haplessly, like going after jungle butterflies with a catcher's mitt—before it is snatched away.

This is where that spot is found: just beyond the village of Foria, in the country of Sierra Leone, in West Africa. On the rim of the continent's western bulge, the country is a tiny shape engulfed by the tiny shapes of Guinea and Liberia. It is so obscure that you may never have heard of it; if you have, you likely know it as the place of lost hands. That is the small fame its war has brought, and as the war burned closer to Foria, as it burned within a few miles, the Kortenhovens put off leaving. They came from Grand Rapids, Michigan. But this had been their home for fourteen years.

To reach there they had flown across the Atlantic, flown to the capital, Freetown. In that city on the coast, on the streets above the estuary that spread—gleaming, listless—into the ocean, the elaborate colonial architecture, the pale stone and wrought-iron rails, stood beside stark office buildings of smooth concrete. It had been nearly two decades since the end of British rule. Freetown could appear a functional place, half quaint, half modern. The airlines had been willing to land there, then.

From the capital the family drove inland. The road cracked and caved and disappeared. Branches hooked across the windshield and wrapped around the hood; the family couldn't see five feet into the forest that crushed inward from either side. Even in a four-wheel-drive, to cross most of the miniature country, to travel a distance less than the span of Massachusetts, took fourteen hours. Boulders blocked the route and bridges didn't exist. To make their way across the creeks they built their own bridges, roping together logs with vines.

They were white. And they were missionaries. But they meant to bring basic health care and safe water as well as Christianity; they felt that the gospel's call to "preach good news to the poor" referred at least as much to reducing poverty on earth as to uplifting the poor in spirit. "You can't spiritualize that passage," Paul, the father, tall, sturdy, and bearded, believed. "You can't just go around telling people Jesus loves you, so everything'll be hunky-dory if you have faith in Him. You can't just tell people this world is not my home. The gospel means action as well as words. The biblical mandate is to treat the whole person, not to divide things into the spiritual and the material. I want to build water systems so little kids will stop shitting themselves to death."

"Lord," he wrote in a booklet of prayers, published by his church back in the States, "Lord, give me a heart that breaks."

Paul and Mary's three skinny blond children—Matthew who was thirteen, Sarah who was almost ten, Aaron who had just turned six—tried the vines for swinging, Sarah's ponytail and long, loose skirt floating through the heavy air, when their parents stopped to rest on that first drive up. And they played at the rubber trees—*real rubber trees*, Sarah thought, cutting at the bark with a Swiss Army knife, expecting to fashion rubber bands and Superballs from whatever substance emerged. She had to settle for white sap. It was Christmas, 1980. When the family arrived in Foria, the cotton trees were shedding their delicate fiber. Above the huts of mud and thatch, and the few squat houses of cement and corrugated metal, the white fluff drifted down through the heat, coating the ground like a layer of snow.

The Kortenhovens' denomination, the Christian Reformed Church, a Calvinist sect based in Grand Rapids, had dispatched ahead of them a sort of roving missionary advance man to help choose a village, to meet with village leaders and negotiate for an unused house where the family would live, to set a metal roof upon it. Their church was sending, too, a few other missionaries into the region around Foria, the most remote in Sierra Leone, and one other couple to Foria itself. Quickly, the advance man left, out from that epicenter of isolation, and gradually the other missionaries would follow him away. But even at the start, there were only a handful of Westerners spread over the territory of the Kuronko. Unable to communicate with the people they now lived among, the Kortenhovens struggled to learn the tribal language, Paul and Mary hiring Samba Koroma for their teacher, Samba the rare villager who'd managed to get several years of schooling at a Catholic mission in a distant town, who knew a bit of English, who spoke at high-speed in all his five languages, so

that *"Ah foh tungh doni doni"*—"say it again very slowly"—was the
first Kuronko sentence Paul learned. For months Aaron could
learn nothing. Friendship, at the age of six, seemed to end forever. He could talk with no village child. "I hate Africa!" he
screamed constantly through the house, high voice holding endless depths of helplessness and grief. "I hate rice! I hate cement!
Why don't we have carpet on the floor? I want to go home to
America! I hate Africa! I want to go home! I want to go home! I
hate rice! Please, why can't we go home?" And at night, with the
kerosene lanterns blown out, they all listened to the termites,
tk-tk-tch, tk-tk-tch, devouring the door frames and the flimsy
wooden substructure supporting their concrete walls.

Was there only an ocean between the country they had come
to and the country they had left? Living beyond electricity, beyond phones, beyond mail seemed the least of it. When Aaron
got sick that first year, when Mary pushed gently at his right side
and the pain was sharp, she figured appendicitis. She and Paul
rushed him to the closest hospital, five hours away. There the
Seventh Day Adventist doctors cared for a colony of lepers. After
he was diagnosed with hepatitis, Aaron recuperated among the
patients whose nerves had been claimed by leprosy's bacteria,
whose eyelids could no longer blink, whose flesh had turned
necrotic, whose hands were crabbed, whose toes had fallen away,
whose feet had eroded to twisted fins.

Back in Foria, school was Mary in tears, leaning over Aaron's
shirtless bony shoulder, trying to teach him to read despite his
dyslexia. Matthew and Sarah studied by way of a University of Ne-
braska correspondence course. They sent off their tests, their papers, whenever anyone journeyed to Freetown. From there the
schoolwork made its way to the States, and made it back to Foria
months later.

And while the termites feasted on the house, cobras and
puff adders, mambas and Gabon vipers—species whose bite, if it
didn't kill, could leave a leg, especially a child's leg, quickly black
with gangrene and treatable by nothing except amputation—

slept by the bathroom drain and slid across the paths. Malaria was rampant, and the drug that fought it gave Aaron hallucinations. Rabies infected the dogs the family took care of for a villager. Elephantiasis was endemic. Lassa fever, with its Ebola-like hemorrhaging, lurked near. They had come to a land of plagues.

Then one night, to make the ocean between countries seem all but infinite, a bush devil danced outside the Kortenhovens' windows. Opposite their house, the village planned to build new huts; a patch of forest needed to be cleared, and before this could begin, devils needed to be purged. They surely lingered amidst those trees, cotton trees and others with trunks so terribly thick and horribly tall, the natural homes of evil spirits when they rose to visit the surface of the earth. For the Kuronko, there was only the magic of peril, not solace, in those fantastic growths, and to step between the buttresses of the cotton trees, to be enfolded by those gargantuan wings, was not to feel ensconced but to guarantee misfortune, disfigurement, sickness, death. The specially sanctified might enter those chambers to leave offerings, sacrifices—colonial coins, chicken's blood—to stave off general disaster. Otherwise the alcoves, so otherworldly, were best avoided. The beings of the underworld felt too at home there.

In a society that was, with only the most scattered exceptions, preliterate, in a territory so besieged by illness that one-third of all children died before the age of five, in a place without any modern sense of science or medicine, in a land so overwhelmed by nature, devils were behind every calamity. Their "witchguns" perpetually cocked, they could shoot anyone with ammunition of hardship. When hunters passed through certain sections of forest, groves favored by the spirits, they never called one another's names, for fear the devils might identify them for later harm. And when the village chief wished to make room for more huts, he first checked the trees for malevolent forces; to cut the trunks before capturing them would be to risk a frenzy of retribution. The entire village could be annihilated.

A bush devil was another figure, not a devil but evil's counterpart, a close cousin to all malign beings, an antidote dangerous in itself, a man inhabited by occult powers that enabled him to do good. Face covered in cloth and body in raffia, he danced with his entourage of spirit-men, danced for hours and hours near the Kortenhovens' house, through the stand of trees; seed-rattlers shook and the *kondeh* gave its cadence and feet stomped rhythmically like a cavalry of hoofbeats, making the ground vibrate. The family was warned to stay inside. All the villagers did the same, kept their shutters closed. Then came the blast of a horn, a tremendous shriek. A devil had been trapped in the forest. With an anguished cry it had surrendered and been expunged.

The woods began to fall. The chopping went on through the next day, stopping only when the cloth face and raffia body returned, suspicious that more evil hid within the trees. Again the villagers ran for their homes, fleeing the exorcism; again the screeching horn, the horrendous cry. Another spirit had been seized. The cutting resumed. A few minutes later, Samba, the language teacher, came by the house. To him, a man of rare education, Mary said, "We heard the horn."

"That was not a horn," Samba taught her. "It was a devil."

That had been the beginning. The end had begun when Joseph Sesay, a Sierra Leonean who had worked for the mission for more than a decade, a self-taught agriculturalist trying to increase the yield of local rice farms and palm groves, ventured south to see how close the war had come. There were rumors that it was near, that the rebels who'd been fighting for three years in the country's southeast had surged north, abruptly bringing their terror, their impaling of civilians and incinerating of villages, into the region around Foria. And the Kortenhovens knew that the Revolutionary United Front wasn't playing by the racial rules that often lend whites a level of immunity in the

worst third-world situations. In the southeast, an American working for the Red Cross had been taken hostage. An Irish priest
and a Dutch missionary couple with their three-year-old daughter had been killed. Yet in Foria, among black and white, there
was fear without extreme panic, isolation blurring the war's reality, and Joseph volunteered to ride his mission Honda toward
Bendugu, twenty miles away, to find out what was truly happening. It was dusk when he left, midnight when he returned, the
great drum sounding its three slow beats followed by staccato
patter, the signal that news had arrived and that the villagers
should assemble. They crowded around the Kortenhovens veranda, and Joseph told what he had done and seen.

The settlements past Alikalia had been all but deserted, and
outside Bendugu he had left his motorbike, stolen quietly along
a footpath, climbed a tree. In the distance scattered homes were
just starting to erupt in kerosene flames. But closer by, maybe a
hundred yards off, he noticed something strange: specks of red
and pink light, variably still and swooping, not far above the
ground.

Later he would learn what the rebels did: stuck candy wrap-
pers on the ends of their flashlights, so they could distinguish
the beams of their comrades from those of any civilians racing to
find family or belongings before trying to escape. But for the
moment he understood so little, only saw the start of conflagra-
tion and the inexplicable dancing of colored lights.

TWO Lamin Jusu Jarka took my arm in his metal claw. He forced me down, doubled me over, pinned my forearm to the long, exposed root of the mango tree. This was later in the war, after the fighting had reached Freetown. He wanted me to know what had happened in his suburb.

As he held me in this way, his country had just been named by the United Nations, for the third year in a row, as the worst on earth. Education and economy and health care all play their parts in such a ranking. The fact that Sierra Leone was being ravaged by what was perhaps the most horrific civil war on a continent of civil war, and that it had been ravaged already for almost a decade, didn't help in any category. Its citizens had a life expectancy of thirty-seven years.

This was the nation I kept traveling to. The questions that drew me, the ones I can articulate, came down to these: Could a place so abject be even partly rescued? Could a society even somewhat functional in modern terms, a society where mere survival was not the overriding order, be built in a country so thoroughly broken, where mere survival was so hard? And could the white Western world carry out the beginnings of such a transformation, succeed on a continent it tended to view as unsalvageable, if, as had suddenly become the case, a mission of rescue was truly launched? Yet there were murkier reasons, too, for the time I devoted to Sierra Leone, reasons far less cogent and impossible to pose as questions, reasons I would often have reached inside myself to eradicate, had they not been lodged too deep, in the psychic region that guards our sense of race, in the irrational province of my white self.

But for the moment, I was there only for Lamin.

"Today," he had thought, opening his front door on the afternoon, in January 1999, when the rebels swarmed through his hillside neighborhood, "is going to be a different day." A soldier stood on the threshold of his small house. A second earlier the man had been knocking, knocking loud and hard with the butt of his rifle. He'd been threatening that if the door wasn't unlocked fast he would fire through it, fire through the windows, fill the house with bullets. Lamin made sure his wife and daughter were out of sight behind a bed. Then, thinking it would be their best chance, thinking with too much fear and too little time for thought, he opened the door. So this father whose bearish face broke often into a warm smile, this former security guard for Barclay's Bank downtown, this forty-one-year-old man who had been—as he put it in his elaborate English learned somehow around the city—"unfortunate to be among the redundancy group" when the war slaughtered the economy, stood facing a young man in jeans and a Tupac Shakur T-shirt, a young man with an AK-47 and a black cap and white drug-frothed saliva webbing the corners of his mouth. "Today"—the thought ran through Lamin's head repeatedly—"is going to be a different day."

The soldier yelled that he would shoot anyone he found inside. Lamin's wife and daughter emerged from the back. Hannah, the daughter, was fourteen. She had large eyes that dominated her slender face, a smooth complexion of soft brown. The man informed Lamin that his first wife had been killed during a battle upcountry. His children, he declared, had been killed, too. He seemed pleased with the ultimate fairness in his finding a pretty girl behind this wooden door. "Oh," he said, sounding almost surprised by the world's great balance, "now I have got my next wife."

He demanded that she follow him up the hill—high above the bay and the dockyards, above the neighborhood that mixed hovels with crude apartment blocks—and back into the jungle. She asked that he wait while she got her slippers.

And meanwhile throughout the area similar weddings were

taking place. Next to a nearby roadblock, a female soldier checked the virginity of her captives, prodding with her fingers after the girls were stripped naked and pinned to the ground. Then she made her suggestions to the senior officers of her unit. And in the city, on the grounds of the State House where the rebels ran a command post, hundreds of young women were rounded up, to be fucked in the offices or on the walkways. Everywhere, hoping to be undesired, the youthful tried to look haggard, and, with mixtures of water and soil and ash, the light-skinned tried to make themselves dark.

Though vehement in his orders, the soldier waited, almost politely, for his due. He didn't follow Hannah into the house as she went to retrieve her slippers, and she, as if quickly accustomed to the rites of this war, seemed to have given in already.

But Lamin managed to turn, to step with her to the back of the house, to urge her out through a bedroom window. He stood again at the door, as if waiting for her. The soldier seemed bewildered, then stunned by the delay. He pointed the assault rifle, clutched at chest height. There were threats, there were pleas. Lamin promised to fetch his daughter. "Don't fire me, don't fire me, don't fire me, don't fire me," he begged countless times before grabbing at the gun. His wife got out in the chaos. Alone, the men danced around the shabby room, attached to each other by their clinging to the rifle. Lamin held the barrel, the soldier gripped the stock. They tried to spin each other, to dip each other to the floor. The dance seemed to last minutes. "Don't fire me, don't fire me," he kept singing. And at last he succeeded, couldn't twist the gun away but sent the man reeling down. Lamin ran outside into the dry-season sun, into the world of billowing flames and littered bodies, the stuttering of AKs.

Marauding soldiers had been lurking at the base of the hill for days, and some of Lamin's neighbors had squeezed themselves into the low concrete tombs of the cemetery; the vaults were poorly made and could be pried open, and now the living hid beside the dead. Others crouched in the dungeon of the psychiatric asylum, a lightless cave beneath the dilapidated, fortress-like hospital; they existed in darkness with the most wildly deranged, the ones they prayed the soldiers might leave alone, while other patients waited, ankles in irons, chained to the floor of the outdoor pavilion. In the next suburb, a science teacher, a timid, reedy man I came to know well, had kept himself and his five-year-old brother alive by letting the soldiers take the neighborhood girls into his house for raping. The teacher was the first in his family to be educated, and the little boy had been sent from upcountry to be raised, the teacher's special charge. But the soldiers grew tired of the house; they set the furniture ablaze and padlocked the door with the brothers inside. Steel bars covered the small windows. The teacher pulled and kicked, cracking the cheap cement around the bars. The five-year-old's lungs filled with smoke; he suffocated before his brother could get them free.

And now fire was everywhere: Torches—raffia mats rolled and soaked in kerosene—ignited home after home; flames ravished the hills; family after family was burned alive.

Lamin sprinted outside, above where a group of children sang. At gunpoint—some of the guns held by children themselves: nine, ten, eleven years old—they clapped their hands and repeated lyrics the rebels taught them:

We want peace
We have come for peace

There had been other songs, other dogmas when the revolutionaries had first made themselves known, years ago. But lately, as they carried out missions code-named "Operation No Living Thing" or "Operation Pay Yourself," they had settled on the purest ideology:

We want peace
We have come for peace

The government army hardly existed. Two years ago it had briefly overthrown the president; now many of its soldiers fought in volatile tandem with the rebels, and many of the rest, by long-standing tradition, took any random opportunity for terror and looting. Plenty of the men and boys sweeping through Lamin's area were government troops, and though their stated objective was better government, their prime enemy seemed to be anyone without a gun, anyone not raping and making mayhem along-side them. All was anarchy. The government of President Tejan Kabbah, such as it was, was defended mostly by a proxy force of Nigerians, dispatched by a dictator with his own reasons, and by a loose alliance of Sierra Leonean hunting societies, militias whose amulets made them immune to bullets. And while the Nigerian army and the inoculated gunmen fought the opposi-tion inside Freetown—tying, flogging, beating, and often execut-ing anyone suspected of rebel sympathy along the way—the rebels and government troops went into an ever-increasing frenzy on the outskirts of the city. They sliced open the bellies of pregnant women, betting on the sex of the fetuses; they stepped up the pace of rape and stoked up the volume of singing; they climbed through Lamin's neighborhood, where he now scram-bled over a dirt embankment and along a shallow ditch and made it as far as the high wall of the asylum.

There a pack of soldiers caught him, some in full camou-flage, some in street clothes, some with American flag bandan-nas tied over their heads or around their necks, and one female commander, pillowed immensely in fat, wearing nothing but a red bra and red panties and black military boots.

As they brought him to the mango tree she hurried every-thing along. A few of the soldiers listened to the people in line, their breathless pleas, their hysterical, hyperventilating voices as they said they had wished for an overthrow all along, claimed they had fought with the rebels last month, last year. She kept the line moving, barked at the soldiers to quit wasting time, screamed that their captives were all "Kabbah's children."

From somewhere on the hill Lamin heard a neighbor cry, "The cut hands people have come, the cut hands people have come!" Later he would discover what the man was doing: Blood running from his stumps, the neighbor staggered through the unpaved streets, trying to taunt the soldiers into killing him. "The cut hands people have come, the cut hands people have come!" But they would not finish him off. They only took a hammer and broke both sides of his jaw.

And elsewhere tiny children, too young to speak, had arms severed at their dimpled elbows, their padded wrists.

The mango tree's roots stretched ten or fifteen feet from the trunk, sprawling aboveground at knee height. In line, Lamin sputtered the name of his tribe, from the upcountry region where the rebels had originated, hoping to win sympathy. He tried to tell them in his tribal language, and in Krio, the patois of the nation. "Brothers," he wailed, the line moving forward. But tribe, in this war, wasn't much of a factor. Half-blind, tears streaming, beyond all self-control, he kept on: "Leave me so I can go with you . . . I am part of you . . . I beg you . . . I am one of you . . . I am with you . . . If you could just say for me to join you . . ."

"Put your mammy ass nyah!"

A soldier seized his arm. Forced him down, doubled him over. Braced his forearm across the root.

The young man straddling the root at the base of the tree wore sneakers, camouflage pants, a white T-shirt markered with his rank and title, "C. O. Cut Hands." Lamin was sobbing, too tearful and afraid to get much glimpse of his face. And he still hoped that if he was respectful, didn't lift his eyes, C. O. Cut Hands wouldn't raise his ax.

"I am with you, I am with you."

The blade crashed through bone, a few inches above Lamin's wrist.

Against the root, his left arm replaced his right.

A white burlap rice sack lay on the ground. Lamin's hands were tossed in.

■ ■ ■

Later, Lamin's neighbors told him that C. O. Cut Hands was a cousin of the boys who lived next door to Lamin's house, that he was a government soldier the neighborhood knew as Sahjunior. My talks with the next-door family, and with people who'd seen the cutting, seemed to bear this out. But no one had much idea why he'd returned in this way to a place where he'd played as a child. One woman remembered some slight, she couldn't be sure exactly what, maybe that he'd been forbidden to take the fruit, or to rest in the shade, of a family tree. As she spoke, the memory seemed as thin as the suggested reason.

"So much nonsense," Lamin said, categorizing what had happened in his neighborhood, in his country, before he gripped my pink forearm between the two steel pincers of his right hand. The move was swift, the pincers exact in their aim, not bumping my hip but clasping my arm so deftly it was almost like the gesture of a seasoned escort, impeccably gentle. Then his heavy chest leaned against my shoulder, his belly against part of my back, and he bent me to the root, my nose near the wood. The gesture hadn't become brutal—it was still too smooth and sudden for that—only overpowering. The pincers were tight and firm, as if mechanically locked. He set my forearm hard against the root, bone feeling wood and bone feeling steel. "As I am doing with you now, just so," he said.

I tugged a bit, but the pincers did not react. I could not get free. "These are the marks," he said, indicating the many blade-thin scars on the root, my face only inches above them. "Look at the stains." And on the rough, mottled surface of tan and dark brown I could just make out darker traces, which might or might not have been blood.

"Can you see?"

I wasn't sure.

I figured he would let me up then. He didn't. The only way I

could get my arm loose was to twist hard, to swing my other fist
up into him. For a moment this seemed necessary. And for the
next several seconds I told myself that I *could*, that surely I was capable of knocking his ruined body backward. The thought was
reassuring. It was essential. It calmed me. Because once, I had
expected that the horror of entering a world like Lamin's would
be in imagining myself as the one with the ax, in closing my eyes
and putting my hand around the handle and bringing the
weapon down. But such imagining was not impossibly hard. The
truly unbearable thing, the thing I needed to feel was impossible, was the opposite: that I could ever be made as helpless as
Lamin had been made, or that my home, my world, could ever
fall so low, could ever feel so lost, so shattered, and so weak as
the world that was his.

The spongy, blood-soaked tissue of his stumps held above his
head, he stumbled back toward his house, though he scarcely
knew where he was going. He made it to the front porch, no farther. His entire circular journey, his odyssey, beginning at the
house with his flight from the gunman and ending where the
gunman had stood, had been about seventy yards. He collapsed,
facedown, blood streaming over the porch.

His wife returned some time later. Motionless on the cement, he watched her come near, her yellow-brown face, her
matching *lappas*, patterned in pink and white and green, flowing
around her small body and wrapped around her head. "Maria,"
he said, though usually they called each other by special nick-
names, just letters, M-A for her, J-U for him. He felt she couldn't
see him, was about to walk by. He tried again, again using her
formal name as if somehow it would make her hear. "Maria."

She took off the *lappa* that clothed her upper body, and covered his forearms, binding them together, hoping to staunch the
blood. Hannah she'd left hiding in another house, but as for the

rest of their children, who'd been off with relatives, she had no idea. There was nothing their parents could do for them. There was so little most parents could do. One neighbor's son had been shot dead near the mango tree. The father, standing over the body, attempted to hold him and say goodbye, though his tongue had just been slashed and he had lost his arms.

The *lappa* saturated with blood, M-A untied it. She took the cloth from her head and bandaged again. She helped him to stand. She held him beneath one arm as they began to walk. They headed downhill toward the two-room shanty of a local surgeon, where they thought they might get bandages, medicine, something. "During that time," he remembered, "I didn't know whether I was still living in this world. During that time when my hands were chopped off, when my blood was pumping, I didn't know. I thought, I have almost gone to the next world. In fact, when my wife managed to get me to Mr. Conteh's Surgery, I thought there was somebody behind my back, somebody walking behind me, pushing me along."

And no, he had not wished to die. For days and days he did not care, but he did not ask for it or pray for it or seek it out. And then the uncaring was over. Mostly. He was a man who had to be fed by his wife, who could not use the bathroom without someone beside him. Yet he decided there were things he had still to accomplish.

THREE "Listennnn to me!"
Sam Rosenfeld, captain in the British army, lifted his arms as though in benediction, spreading his white hands high and wide above the thousand black soldiers who knelt in the mud before him. He bellowed his words, and the black men yelled in reply, "Listen to de white man!" The scene, in the summer of 2000, appeared to rise out of the nineteenth century, and the Krio-flavored speech seemed to compound the reversal of time.

I had come for this, the rescue. Before I set out to learn from the lives of the people I will tell you about, people like the Kortenhovens and Lamin, or like the mercenary soldier and the medical student with the cure for HIV, before I had learned much of anything, I began following the British, who had arrived to "sort out" their former colony.

That was the phrase they used for putting things right, and it was strange, because at the time, in their minds, they seemed to have everything sorted out already: Evil was embodied in the Revolutionary United Front, the R.U.F., the rebels whose founding leader was an ex-wedding photographer named Foday Sankoh, his motives simply greed and power, his army equipped through profits from smuggled diamonds and manned by children taken captive and forced, for the purposes of initiation, to hack off the limbs of their own parents, his scheme, in part, to terrorize the country into submission, into supporting his "movement" in exchange for mere safety. Salvation was largely a matter of stamping the rebels out. You couldn't see a state of chaos much more clearly, much more sorted out, than that.

In any case, the country, with its five million people, had reached new levels of despair. After Lamin and thousands and thousands of others had lost their arms or legs or ears or lips or eyes or lives around Freetown in January 1999, peace had been negotiated with the rebels and government soldiers allied with them. But the United Nations troops in charge of keeping that peace—about 10,000 armed men, the largest U.N. force anywhere in the world—cowered at the next surge of anarchy. They surrendered their guns and armored vehicles to the rebels; hundreds let themselves be taken hostage; and the U.N.'s central command was so hapless it sometimes had no clue where those battalions of hostages were being held. "We don't have a good idea of where they are," the U.N.'s Freetown spokesman acknowledged about 300 of its soldiers, who'd been missing for weeks. "And we haven't had for some time. All we know is that they're somewhere in Sierra Leone."

So in May 2000—under U.K. authority, safe from U.N. ineptitude—the British landed 800 commandos and anchored warships with battle-ready aircraft off the coast. They kept the capital from being overrun as it had been a year earlier. It didn't take much. The commandos beat back a nighttime assault by the rebels, a test attack near the airport outside the city. The gunfire ended quickly: a few enemy bodies left on the road, the rest vanished into the forest, the British without a bruise. The rebels pulled back a bit, seemed to have learned a lesson. The British patrolled the Freetown streets. They patrolled an area of villages beyond. Their intelligence units guided a raid that freed a contingent of 230 U.N. captives. And Prime Minister Tony Blair decided that Sierra Leone would become an emblem—possibly the most striking emblem—of the "moral dimension" so emphasized in his foreign policy, of his insistence that the West commit itself to solving the world's worst and most violent humanitarian crises, that his country not follow the pattern of the United States, that Britain's mark upon the world be shaped by morality, not circumscribed by strategic self-interest. Britain would do what the United States tended to disdain: It would nation-build.

It would save Sierra Leone. It would start by creating an army that would drive evil out through the jungle. It would take the government military—part of which, commanded by a suddenly born-again Christian general, Johnny Paul Koroma, had lately broken ties with the R.U.F. and announced its renewed allegiance to the president—and it would transform the soldiers into unswayably loyal, ethical, efficient troops who would destroy the rebels. That some of those soldiers had taken full part in the war's atrocities didn't seem to matter. The problem wasn't seen as extensive. Somehow the British would weed out the war criminals. Or, through vigorous training, and through the moral teaching of the British military chaplain, the British would reclaim them. The new Sierra Leone Army would carry out a kind of crusade against the R.U.F. It would make sure nothing like what had happened to Lamin would happen to anyone in this country again.

Today, the weapons instruction would begin with a primal display of British superiority. Swelled with high purpose, Captain Rosenfeld boomed through the end-of-the-world rain that besieged the jungle clearing: "Welcome to the Royal Firepower Demonstration!"

The throng of soldiers was rapt. Whatever they had done in the past, they seemed anxious now for order, in their army, in their nation, or eager simply to associate themselves with British power. And the country seemed ready to be re-made—or reel backward. "Welcome back, our colonial masters," government officials had greeted the British force when it arrived. "Are you here to set our country straight?" The question held no irony. The hope seemed universal. A street seller taught me with a parable: "If you are traveling by boat, and the boat turns, and another boat comes so you do not drown—so the British. We have a savior." A soldier explained, "They colonize us. They are our fathers. They know the job perfectly. They know how to discipline us." And when I pressed, when I protested, when I all but ap-

pealed for racial resentment or historical embitterment or at
least some slight worry about the past returning, my driver, Foday Conteh, whom I argued with daily, and who spent our hours
together trying to help me understand what I must have seemed
too dense to absorb, attempted again to school me:

"Now, end of the day, look at we—no light, no proper education, everything finished in Sierra Leone. You get me clear?"
Foday was always concerned about the clarity of his English, his
fourth language. "When we ask independence we can't do it. We
can do nothing here, only go down, only spoil. Railroad train,
factory making. Hah! Where can you see factory now? Oh,
Africa. If the British think about the past, about we cry for independence, I don't think they help us, I don't think they agree.
But all the same, the father is the father. So we bless him. We cry
back for him. End of the day, we cry back for Britain to take back
the country."

Sierra Leone longed to be recolonized.

"We start with the AK-47," Rosenfeld called out in Gortex fatigues. The downpour, which had scarcely stopped for days,
turned the sloping field into a broad river of sinkholes and small
cascades, a bath of water-borne diseases. The trainees wore flip-
flops or went barefoot. Few wore the prized black boots the
British had dispensed, because they owned no socks and their
feet would blister; the British put socks on their list of equipment to supply. The men did have on their newly issued green
ponchos over their own assortment of gym shorts and T-shirts
featuring Betty Boop or the slain rapper Tupac or the beatific
Titanic lovers, Leonardo DiCaprio and Kate Winslet.

"The weapon fires a seven-sixty-two round. Note the banana
magazine holding thirty rounds. This is the way *not* to fire this
weapon!"

Behind the captain on the firing range, one of his team
sprayed bullets wildly, holding the assault rifle at the hip—a
preferred stance in Sierra Leone, where the soldiers studied

Rambo, whose heroics showed constantly in the nation's video shacks.

"As you can see, this achieves nothing but a lot of noise!"

Then the weapon was held and aimed correctly, the U.K. soldier first standing, then kneeling, then lying on his belly in the muck. A concise series of *cracks* reverberated below the surrounding hills of lavish green, and the distant target, a pile of rocks and bricks at least a football field away, was destroyed, made almost to disappear. Enemy lines—if lines existed in this war—were not far behind those hills.

A deep murmur rose from the trainees, the sound long and guttural and straight from the most stereotypical native crowd scene produced by some old Hollywood studio.

Having shown them how they should have been using their corroded AKs, Rosenfeld's team repeated the lesson—blind fire, annihilating aim—with the fresh British rifle all would receive the next morning.

The captain spread his arms again, lifted his hands again. His beret drenched, his face was soft and long eyelashes wet in a way that made him faintly pretty as well as handsome. But his voice was indomitable. *"We will teach you to do that! You will be a fighting force!"*

He was twenty-six years old. He had grown up adoring *Top Gun*, dreamed of becoming an ace pilot, then decided "I want to lead men," and so chose the army instead of the solitary maneuvers of the air. This was the first time he'd been in Africa. But when his outfit, the First Battalion of the Royal Irish Regiment, was sent over to Sierra Leone, he was put in charge of the instruction. His orders left him sleepless for one night. Yet the captain was a supremely confident man. By morning he had "broken the problem down," and in the mess tent he related his outlook to me: "All they need is a bit of professional training from the people who know best. And we are the best at this. It's buck cheese to us." Then he talked with the sweet eagerness of youth about why he was here, about "moral responsibility," his country's and his own and the feeling of responsibility he would instill in his trainees "to protect civilians and protect the civilian government."

And with such security, the democratic leadership of President Kabbah—for despite the war, Sierra Leone had managed to hold multi-party elections back in 1996, a nearly unique event in national history—would start to thrive. When Tony Blair's foreign secretary, Robin Cook, promised to "rebuild Sierra Leone," he was not offering aid on the magnitude of a Marshall Plan for the country, something many advocates for the continent felt should be done throughout Africa. (They wanted it, especially, for the region loosely called "sub-Saharan Africa" and referred to when people spoke of the continent's troubles in general. The region excluded the Mediterranean rim nations. It included —according to those U.N. rankings, known as the Human Development Index—the next twenty-seven worst-off countries directly above Sierra Leone.) Blair himself was about to push hard for multi-national commitment to massive increases in African assistance. But what his foreign secretary was promising, here, was an intensive and steadfast intervention, probably unmatched elsewhere on the continent, that would bring peace and then "good governance." The phrase stood for the most current theory on uplifting the woeful nations of the planet. To construct accountable and sturdy governmental institutions would facilitate private development, and would ensure that aid money benefited the people rather than vanishing in corruption and waste.

The institution of the military, one that guaranteed peace and obeyed elected authority, would be the starting point in Sierra Leone. Yet even as that project began, the British were laying a broader foundation. They didn't intend to recolonize, but already, in addition to their colonels taking leadership over the army, they'd sent, at Kabbah's request, a former deputy police chief from Kent to head the government's police force (in the few areas the government controlled well enough to field a police force). And an English accountant was overseeing the government's finances as accountant general, searching out corruption (little search was needed) and trying to get control of mysterious spending and introduce the idea of transparency. The plan was to revamp in emergency while teaching by example. The goal was to foster, in Sierra Leone, an open and democratic society on a continent of dictatorship and collapsed states, a continent where one-fifth of the population lived amidst civil war—a statistic that didn't begin to include mere deadly unrest. Africa, Blair announced, was "a scar on the conscience of the world." Sierra Leone would be proof that the scar could be healed.

Now Rosenfeld's team fired a sequence of light and heavy machine guns, mounted on bipods and trucks. The vibrations churned through chest and groin. The skin of my pelvis felt like a drumhead.

"This weapon is effective at eighteen hundred meters," the captain yelled. "As you can see, it takes a few moments to put into action. But its results are devastating."

British instructors plugged their ears with their fingers; the trainees simply gazed at the range where, within seconds, countless perfectly aimed rounds caused the targets to disintegrate, reduced them to billows of smoke. The crowd was standing, their guttural murmur turning to a huge, exultant roar. Framed by the ring of hills, Rosenfeld commanded his men to unleash the mortars. They decimated patches of jungle. Nothing but great smoke clouds remained. *"We will teach your support platoons to do that! When your battalions plan to attack, that is the support they will give you! Just imagine the enemy fear before you even get there!"* The rain was diminishing as if on British cue. The mist crept up toward the ridges. "Hey, R.U.F. rebel!" the beginnings of the new Sierra Leone Army called out, laughing, conjuring enemy bases on the hillside where the shells exploded.

"We are the Irish S.L.A.!" they cried.

"Train hard, fight easy!"

"We are going to fuck them up!"
"Kill, kill, kill, kill!"
"Long live the British!"

It had all begun, as perhaps every story of black and white in some way does, with the slave trade, with the twelve million sent across the Atlantic, with the millions more who died on their way out of the African interior. They had been seized, originally, in tribal wars, or in barter between clans, the starving selling their people in order to subsist. An unknowable number had served already as slaves to other Africans, on a continent where slavery, in forms almost benign or ritualistically brutal, was widespread (and where, in places like Sierra Leone, it would remain prevalent well into the twentieth century). And plenty of the millions had been taken in raids carried out precisely because, on the coast, there were whites wanting to buy blacks, whites who would pay in cloth or liquor or guns, whites who then shackled their purchases together, ankle to ankle, and packed them into the holds of their ships, holds often so tight and low the bodies were doubled over, so that those who died during the weeks or months of crossing sometimes froze in a rigor mortis of hunched contortions.

"The air soon became unfit for respiration, from a variety of loathsome smells, and brought on a sickness among the slaves, of which many died," Olaudah Equiano, a slave who managed to buy his freedom, wrote of his voyage. "This wretched situation was again aggravated by the galling of the chains, now become insupportable; and the filth of the necessary tubs, into which the children often fell, and were almost suffocated. The shrieks of the women, and the groans of the dying, rendered the whole scene of horror almost inconceivable."

By the eighteenth century, the height of the commerce, more slaves were headed to British colonies than anywhere else in the world. And British ships dominated the business.

Yet England was confused about the blacks on its own soil. It barred them from learning any trade, and so kept them subservient or unemployed, yet it saw itself as a haven of universal liberty. Judicial decisions, rendered as early as 1706, and reversed and affirmed repeatedly in a legal war between colonial planters and abolitionists, declared slavery illegal within England and ruled that blacks brought to the country by their owners were permanently free the minute they stepped onto England's piers. English air, one justice declaimed, was "too pure" for slavery.

And while the British read bestselling accounts like Equiano's, and while they read newspaper articles about the captain of the English ship *Zong* forcing his human cargo overboard for the sake of an insurance claim, they confronted, in the late eighteenth century, a black population growing larger and more problematic, partly because black loyalists of the American Revolution had come to London seeking manumission and— unsuccessfully—compensation from the country they'd fought for. Quickly destitute, their vagrancy and begging upset the city and threatened the white poor whose jobs they might take. It was in this air of white guilt and revulsion and fear that Granville Sharp, one of Britain's pivotal white abolitionists, religiously inspired and intellectually eccentric, conceived a utopia on the west coast of Africa. It would be populated by England's blacks. It would be governed according to Sharp's pet notion: frankpledge, an eleventh-century Norman system whereby small groups of households took legal responsibility for one another's conduct. It would be structured around the exchange of labor rather than the evils of money. And this immaculate village would prove to everyone the civility of the black race. "God hath made of one blood all nations of men," Sharp pronounced, quoting scripture. His "Province of Freedom" would be home to "the freest and happiest people on earth."

So, with the backing of a government anxious for ways to handle its black indigents, about 350 blacks, along with around twenty white craftsmen to help get the settlement built and five white doctors to keep it well, sailed away from England in 1787. For reasons unrecorded, seventy white prostitutes were also on board, and together they headed for the West African peninsula that had been named Sierra Leone (either for the leonine shape of its hills or the roar of its thunder) by a Portuguese explorer in 1462. Since 1562 British slavers had been docking there. And in 1786, only a year before Sharp's dream was launched, the place had been deemed too disease-ridden to hold a British prison colony. "There would not be two people alive in six months," the House of Commons had been told, and the convicts were sent instead to Australia.

The settlers landed and were lost. Within a year of their reaching Sierra Leone, Sharp, who had stayed in London, continuing on with his activism, learned that only 130 remained. Between violent rains and implosive incompetence, the idyllic farming community he'd envisioned had failed to grow any crops. The settlers had been forced to barter away their clothing and guns for rice from the local Temne. Malaria, typhoid, yellow fever, and starvation had killed them. Of those who survived, many had gone off to work in the best business around: the slave trade.

The new slavers included blacks as well as almost all the whites Sharp sent to Sierra Leone on a second, supplemental, voyage. Henry Demane, whose emancipation from a colonial planter Sharp had personally engineered back in Britain, became one of the wealthiest. "He is now in danger," Sharp wrote in admonition to those still living in his utopia, "of eternal slavery!" And meanwhile the settlers burned down the village of the Temne king, and the king sent his people to do the same to the settlers. "I have had but melancholy accounts," Sharp grieved, "of my poor little ill-thriven swarthy daughter, the unfortunate colony of Sierra Leone."

Yet the colony took strength when Britain resolved on a broad crusade: to end the slave trade altogether. In 1808—the year

Sierra Leone came under official rule of the British crown—English patrols began intercepting slave ships of all nations off the African shore. The English captains were paid by the number of blacks they reclaimed, and by mid-century about 50,000 had been brought to the colony (which, at the time, included only the territory around present-day Freetown). There the British deposited all the "recaptives." There they were put under the governance of white missionaries who ran villages christened with British names like Regent and Hastings. The villages were supported by the devout in England: for five pounds, a newly freed African would be baptized with the name of the donor.

Others who'd been rescued from the slavers were corralled in a central square and chosen for "apprenticeship" by settlers and earlier recaptives. They were caned if their work was poor, shackled if they tried to escape. Or they were sold as slaves to up-country tribes. "Africans, your King desires you to be free, and to keep others free!" one freshly arrived British governor railed. The colony's governors were (with the exception of one West Indian military doctor) always white.

But for all its racial hypocrisy, for all its stratified brutality, the colony was a kind of melting pot, its streets filled with the Fula in their robes and the British in their suits and the Kroo in next to nothing and the creolized society of recaptives in clothes more emphatically European than the British they emulated: in top hats and spats, in suits of wool because it was considered more English than cotton. And because of the white missionaries, borne in hammocks by their black converts, Sierra Leone became a unique outpost of European-style education in West Africa. By the 1860s, Sierra Leonean children went to school at higher rates than children in Britain. Fourah Bay College, founded by missionaries in a grand building at the waterside, sent its best students on to study in England. The colony produced lawyers and doctors. Samuel Lewis, son of a Yoruba recaptive, became an attorney retained by British businessmen, hired by the governors of Sierra Leone, elected mayor of Free-

town, and named, by Queen Victoria, the realm's first African
knight.

There was, on Western terms, an attempt to uplift. But that
attempt became more and more mixed, toward the end of the
nineteenth century, with conquest and commerce as the European powers divided up Africa for imperial rule. Competing
against French expansion, Freetown annexed inland territory
(up to today's borders) in 1896. It secured its access to the raw
materials England needed, mostly palm oil for soap, industrial
lubricants, and the glycerin used in explosives. It taxed its new
subjects as a way to raise their production of palm oil; it put
down their rebellions, cutting them apart with the new Maxim
machine gun; and always it spoke of civilizing, of enlightening,
its campaigns of enforcement undertaken not only for the sake
of domination and trade but for purging the interior tribes of
cannibalism and slavery.

Whether or not the uplifting of Sierra Leoneans remained a
real priority as the age of imperialism took full hold, elevating
them to positions of authority was not a prime ambition. The
increased aggression of the era went along with increased arrogance and distrust. In 1892, close to half the colony's senior
administrators were Sierra Leonean; by 1912, the figure was
one-sixth.

And by the early 1950s—when world war had strengthened,
throughout the continent, movements for self-determination;
when the currents toward Europe's letting go had grown more
powerful than the reasons for clinging on—the fraction was still
around one-fifth. Sierra Leone's independence in 1961 came
without much fight, without Ghana's cataclysmic riots and liberation leaders kept in prison, without the warfare that raged
through Kenya. But the colony's metamorphosis came with violent speed. By 1960, the British had raced to put Sierra
Leoneans into three-fifths of the colony's upper administration,
as though a tradition of modern self-government could be created in less than a decade.

"On 27th April, 1961, Sierra Leone will become independent," a British government booklet, *Sierra Leone: The Making of a Nation*, informed in the months before the ceremony. "The event will mark the fulfillment in Sierra Leone of the United Kingdom's policy in its dependencies of working in partnership with the local people to build up new nations, capable of making their own way in the world. . . . As the people have gained political experience, more and more authority has been transferred to them until now the territory has a very large measure of responsibility for its own affairs."

A sense of responsibility did in fact prevail in the new nation's leadership for about three years, a system of democracy for about six. Then came twenty-nine years of successive dictatorships, of mismanagement so thorough and corruption so complete that the government no longer had any regular revenue, was propped up almost entirely by international aid, and paid its civil servants so infrequently that they looted their own offices, selling off their typewriters and desks and light fixtures to feed their families. Everything that Britain had, in reality, bequeathed to Sierra Leone—decent schools, decent roads, dependable electricity—was, by the mid-1990s, gone. The unpaid teachers sold exam scores; the unpaid education officials sold secondary school placements and professional school degrees; the unmaintained roads had given way to impassable craters; and, except where private generators made for specks of light, the capital, every evening, became a place of total darkness.

One morning I visited one of Sierra Leone's former dictators. To find him I rode with Mike Kpukumu, who'd served as the dictator's chief of security, and who now planned to employ his Liberian agricultural degree in selling organic fertilizer to the government. He and his American partner, an ex-sports bet tout from Las Vegas, needed only enough bribed officials to get their business going.

Mike spoke plainly about the time he and the dictator had spent together before they made their coup, fighting the R.U.F. at the start of the war, in the early '90s, with the government army. "Daniel," he said, "the only good soldier is a dead soldier." He laughed at his line, sounded cheerful, at first. "We are all mothahfuckahs. You see a soldier, he has not had a woman for six or seven weeks, I will show you the raping. He has not eaten, the looting begins. The hungry man becomes bitchy. There is no pay, no food, no system, no sense of belonging. You become a bitch."

Mike was equally clear about the British. Unlike almost all Sierra Leoneans, he put no faith in them—and in the white race. His opinions ran a long way from the lectures of my driver, Foday. "It's the black man," Foday would analyze the state of Sierra Leone, the rueful state of Africa. "The black man witchcraft, it only for spoil. You get me? You know 'spoil'?" Near where Lamin had lost his hands, Foday's mother and son had been killed. A grenade had been launched into the mother's home by a government soldier who called himself Captain Blood. Meanwhile a man named Burn Trouble had been making a list, asking "Long sleeve, short sleeve?"—giving Foday the choice of having an arm cut off at the wrist or shoulder when an amputation squad reached his house. This, anyway, he had avoided. "The white man witchcraft, you are make something to better the world. Planes. Ships. This now." He referred to a bottle of Coke.

I heard the faith everywhere, a hundred versions of what Lamin told me—"You people who are white have got more superpower to train the devil"—or what a bartender upcountry explained of the national ruin all around us: "It's the black man, the typical black man. I'm telling you."

"You know that white people do plenty of things that are just as terrible," I said.

"Look at this country."

"Look at Mali," I named a nearby nation of fair stability.

"Look at Liberia. Look at Congo."

"White people are just as terrible. You're wrong if you don't believe that."

"I don't know what it is," he ignored me. "It's in the skin. You, the white, is different." He rubbed his lustrous brown forearm. "It will take a long time to get rid of this."

Not long before I went with Mike to meet the ex-dictator, the national stadium had filled for a praise rally in honor of the British, placards imploring them to be master again. "Over my dead body," Mike said, driving out of Freetown, away from the glittering beach where the fishermen hauled in their catch in gargantuan hand-woven nets, away from the burnt-out wreckage of the houses, the charred cavern of the City Life Bakery, the rubble of the Treasury Building, whose half-remaining ground floor rooms served as vast latrines, and out past the festooning of seared car skeletons, still vaguely colorful in their reds and blues, lining the sides of the road. "We hate ourselves in Sierra Leone. But let me tell you, in the first place we were made into slaves. And the advent of colonial rule—some of us who have been to school, we know the impact it had."

And now, he went on, the British had waited to stage their rescue "until every one of us is dead," his incredulous, angry words blending with a thought I sometimes had, that the British had left their colony in a hurry and returned at the last minute in heroic storm to prove that Africans had needed the white man's civilizing influence all along.

The ex-dictator had the somewhat extravagant name of Valentine. Valentine Strasser. "When you approach the lion's den," Mike prepared me, "you must bring him gifts. He is a former head of state, used to his choice of dishes. If you want to leave with your head, you'd better bring him something." Mike himself never visited without an offering; today he suggested a fifty-kilo bag of rice, worth about fifteen dollars. I said that would be fine. But before we turned off the main road and onto a dirt track, away from the U.N. roadblocks with their machine guns and sandbags, he stopped at a sprawling shed. Here bald tires and redated cans of sardines were sold by a family of Lebanese, merchant people of Sierra Leone since the late nineteenth century. Mike told me to buy six cans of Holsten beer, total price $3.50, and two packs of Fifty-Five cigarettes for $1 each. With these, he said, the former head of state would be pleased.

When Strasser had taken power, in 1992, at the age of twenty-six, his coup had been well-received. (Mike said he'd found little but condoms in the drawers of the presidential office, which the previous ruler had just fled.) And Strasser's presidency, which had lasted four years, was still seen as one of the country's best. True, he'd made the mistake of freeing convicts and dragooning street kids in order to build the government army from 3,000 to more than 10,000, and this had helped build the national military tradition of "sobels" (who transmogrified from soldiers to rebels and back again, depending on the chances for pillaging). And true, Amnesty International had decried the summary execution of his rivals. But he'd also cleaned the refuse from Freetown's trash-laden streets and almost cleared the R.U.F. from the country. He'd carried out the beautification by declaring Cleaning Saturdays and dispatching his soldiers, twelve years old and up, to make sure people spent their Saturday mornings in virtue, sweeping inside and outside their houses and shanties. (Years later, without much enforcement, Cleaning Saturdays were still observed.) The brief triumph in the war he'd accomplished by hiring 200 mercenaries from South Africa. These had been two of the greatest achievements in national history.

We climbed up into the forest, up past the open-air clinic of a doctor who treated his tuberculosis patients with a rub of ground leaves, taken from a tree where he'd left kola nuts and bits of yarn. He had leaves for cancer and *akobo*, impotency, as well. Strasser's home, a small villa, was in a clearing above a foggy creek. It was cradled by plush round mountains. The villa had been pocked by hundreds of bullets across its once-white façade, and an adjacent house had been missing its roof since a Nigerian bomber had flown over. But the spot was beautiful. Human ruin could do nothing to this landscape, where a predatory bird, elegant as an eagle, floated down and landed, claws out, on rough palm bark. And though the rooms of the lion's den were bare as caves, and though he lived alone except for his mother, whose slippers echoed along distant corridors, the ex-dictator was as fastidious as ever. He'd patched each of the hundreds of bullet holes with a tiny dab of mud.

In jeans and a camouflage T-shirt with cutoff sleeves, he slouched, that morning, in a decrepit cane chair on a wide veranda. Within the expanse defined by the railing's curved balustrades, that chair was the only piece of furniture. And besides Mike and me, Strasser was the only person in sight. He didn't seem to have any bodyguards, any armed boys idling here and there, and at night, Mike told me, he slept not in the villa but on a military cot off in the forest, to thwart the hunt of old enemies. He greeted us without rising, took a slug from a bottle of whiskey called Diplomat. He told us to place the beer, the six gold-tinted cans, at his feet.

Mike had been right. The offering was well received. Immediately Strasser opened up, commencing a two-hour rapid-fire monologue ranging from his certainty that Kabbah would institute *shariah* law to his memories of selfless rule ("Did I tell them to put my face on the new bills they were printing? Did I act with grandiosity and fucking self-aggrandizement? Did I, when the World Bank asked whose face I wanted? Mike will tell you. I did not act in such a fucking way . . .") to his recent mistreatment at the hands of "the U.N. *dog*!" and "the British *dog*!" and above all "the Nigerian *dog*!" whose soldiers had stopped by the villa earlier that very morning to question him and kick him in the shins. "The dogs will be slain! Mike, you tell him." He sprang from his chair and shadow-boxed with lean strong arms. "The dogs will be fucking slain!" But mostly the ex-president, once the youngest head of state in the world, wanted to discuss his grades.

After Strasser's rule had ended with him in handcuffs in a

bloodless coup, the United Nations had kept him from stirring trouble by agreeing to fly him off to England and enrolling him at Warwick University. He'd flunked out, winding up on the dole before winding his way back to Sierra Leone. Meanwhile, he'd adopted a variable British accent, the particular region unclear, lost within the tremendous and distorting stress he put on his British syllables. "Fucking" became "fohking" and "soldiers" gathered a hard "d" and lost its "e" to become "sohldrs" and "your" became "yourn" and it all added up to his own brogue. In it, he complained of the "fohking" teachers who failed to teach and the "fohking" grades that hadn't been fair and "the fohking U.N. dog" who took his scholarship and left him "studying sweet nothing." He was shadow-boxing like crazy, occasionally leaning, with narrow face and flinty eyes, tight to where I sat on the veranda's rail, and sometimes pointing at my chin, so that I felt a minor concern that I'd taken on dog status as well. But he slumped back down in his chair, a teenager suspended from school, wronged and sulking. "I told them what business is it of yourn, my *fohking* grades?"

Abruptly, then, he picked up the four-page Freetown newspaper Mike had presented along with the beer and cigarettes. He began reading. Our audience was over. It ended regally, without warning, the flimsy paper raised in front of his face as though he'd swept from a fabulous room.

Shortly after Strasser had been deposed, Tejan Kabbah had been voted in, the ballot-counting not quite fair but, given the circumstances, declared by international observers to be fair enough. Upcountry, in the weeks before election day, village attacks and amputations increased, the message being that others would have their hands hacked off if they used them to mark a ballot slip at all.

So the nation had a democratic president, one whose public

résumé consisted solely of "ex-U.N. Official." That was all the people knew of Kabbah, no post that he'd held, no program he'd overseen. "Ex-U.N. Official" was more than enough. It must have sounded wonderfully innocuous amidst what the country was going through.

The difficulty was that Kabbah lived up to his blank bureaucratic past, hiding with his votes in the Presidential Lodge, high on a guarded hill, scarcely to be seen again. He fled to Guinea during the overthrow of '97, returned to invisibility when he was restored. "Not exactly charismatic," as the United States ambassador once told me, and apparently petrified, the president would not emerge, even during periods when Freetown was buffered from threat. "I think I've been outside more than he has," the ambassador smiled. His joke was that the ever-cautious U.S. government wouldn't let its ambassador venture outdoors at all, except to ride in his armored van between his residence and the embassy.

If Strasser's legacy was Cleaning Saturdays, Kabbah's was soon being made at Freetown's scruffy colonial-era golf club, where, when things in the capital got rough, the eighth hole bunker doubled as a machine gun post, but where, as soon as the fighting drifted back to thirty or so miles outside, play carried on for those who could afford it: U.N. staff and aid workers and the Sierra Leonean elite. The president didn't leave home to golf, but his name was often invoked on the course. To "Kabbah" a putt was to get nervous, to strike the ball much too timidly, to fall way short.

In July of '99, the treaty Kabbah negotiated with Foday Sankoh granted the rebel leader high stature in the government. In fairness, Kabbah had good reason to feel that power-sharing was the only way. The death of Nigeria's ruler suddenly threatened that country's military support, and meanwhile the United States had sent Jesse Jackson to convince Kabbah to reconcile. The Clinton administration would commit little money let alone

any troops to stabilize Sierra Leone; the memory of downed helicopters and gruesome death in Somalia had not faded. But
the administration appeared desperate to avoid another mass
slaughter like the one it had looked away from in Rwanda, which
would lead to another round of accusations that it was indiffer-
ent to Africa and that its indifference, when compared to U.S.
engagement in the Balkans, seemed to have plenty to do with
race. So "Papa" Sankoh, who many human rights advocates considered the worst war criminal in the world, became, with special
vice-presidential status, Chairman of the Commission for the
Management of Strategic Resources, National Reconstruction,
and Development. That is, he was now officially in charge of the
diamond mines he'd until then had to fight to control, the
mines that supplied his army with cocaine and amphetamines,
rifles and grenade launchers.

"We are fighting for a new Sierra Leone, a new Sierra Leone
of freedom," Sankoh had written in his manifesto, sometime after starting his revolution in 1991. He'd been, before then, a cor-
poral in the government army, a prisoner for plotting a coup, an
itinerant photographer in the provinces, a guerilla-trainee under Muammar Qaddafi. "We are fighting for democracy and by
democracy we mean equal opportunity and access to power to
create wealth through free trade, commerce, agriculture, industry, science and technology. Wealth cannot be created without
power. Power cannot be achieved without struggle. And by struggle, we mean the determination, the humanistic urge to remove
the shame of poverty, hunger, disease, squalor, illiteracy, loafing
and hopelessness from this African land of Sierra Leone . . . This
is our vision for the period of the second liberation of Sierra
Leone. Our mission therefore is to contribute to the task of total
political and economic liberation and unification of Africa."

How sincere had he ever been? Had he really cherished
grand ideological dreams or only put on, as most outsiders
seemed to believe, a cheap political costume to conceal his self-

enrichment at the mines or a deranged lust for absolute authority? It was impossible to say, and perhaps it no longer mattered.
A few months after signing the accord with Kabbah, the new diamond czar walked into a rally, escorted by U.N. peacekeepers.
Moon-faced and white-bearded, a sweet grandfather, he blew
kisses to the crowd of soldiers—his own, the government's. He
wore a black-and-white striped robe above rakish snakeskin
boots dyed to match, and on the dais he sat beside his sometime
ally, the government army commander Johnny Paul Koroma,
who wore a pith helmet. There were Christian prayers and Muslim prayers and the soldiers sang "Tell Papa God thank ye." At
last Papa Sankoh stood to speak. "You, sisters and brothers, are
my babies," he told the cheering, jumping throng, some of
whom his army had kidnapped at the age of five or six. He
waited for them to calm down. Then he brushed the fingers of
his right hand across the back of his left. Brushing, brushing. He
smiled beneficently. "You have nothing," he assured all the soldiers, meaning that he'd wiped their hands clean, that they
would never be prosecuted, that the treaty he'd negotiated had
given them—as well as Sankoh himself—amnesty for all they'd
done.

They cheered more loudly, like an assembly of schoolboys
told their peccadillos would go unpunished. And in less than a
year they were maiming again and ensnaring battalions of U.N.
hostages, perhaps because Sankoh was unsatisfied with his government position, or perhaps because the gunmen were beyond
his control.

"The worst thing the British have ever done," Sergeant Terry
Furlong, one of Rosenfeld's team, said with green eyes pained
above a sharp cleft chin, "was take over the empire." At
Benguema, a ramshackle army base, he was taking a break between teaching the trainees to care for their new British rifles, to

adjust the gas regulator and get the weapon going again fast in case it stopped in battle. "The second worst thing was giving it back."

Atonement and arrogance and compassion ("I was stunned by what little people have," Furlong described his first days. "I had to desensitize slightly") ran deep through the British effort, and fueled the mission's optimism, its relentless sense of hope. "This is a tremendous experiment," Captain Fergus Smith, the British spokesman, said, foreseeing peace and, with close British guidance, a chance at flourishing and resilient democracy. "This could be a blueprint." It could show the way for more missions. It would stand as an alternative to the West's inertia during Rwanda's genocide. It might show that Africa—a continental "bottomless pit" of violence and catastrophe, "impossible to get under control," Richard Holbrooke, United States Ambassador to the United Nations, had once lamented to me the dominant Western attitude—could be turned around.

Could it possibly work? Just here, in this one desperate nation? Sometimes I thought it would. And sometimes I thought it had to. I thought this when I watched Lamin, in a camp for amputees, put on his forearms in the morning and walk his five-year-old daughter, Rugiatu, to school, her little fingers wrapped around his metal hand. And I thought this when I stood on the shore—where the moon cast a swath of turquoise across the water, the band widening toward the beach and turning the sand to tinsel—and had the feeling that if the British did not succeed, then Sierra Leone would be cut eternally adrift, would become some sort of netherworld, not connected to the thriving places of the earth by water but condemned to exist as a separate planet, soon to be completely forgotten, because there was nothing else to do but forget. The people in that land would be damned forever to lives nearly unendurable. Yet to be immersed in the country was to feel that it was—already—almost utterly cut off, for it was, in many ways, so raw, so primitive. I use those words knowing how meaningless they may be, how they may speak only of my own inability to see as I should. But I will stick with those words just the same.

Sierra Leone still had its aspects of modernity, of course. From the capital I could send, on most days, an e-mail home to New York. But in the capital I also spent time with a teenager who had lately fought for two factions and eaten human heart and liver.

FOUR

Komba Gbanya had been with the R.U.F., and with a sometime government and sometime rebel militia called the West Side Boys; he'd done "beaucoup killing, beaucoup-beaucoup" on Lamin's hillside during that orgy of burning and amputation. Before his years as a young soldier, he'd built toy cars from strips of cane. He'd constructed sturdy, all-terrain vehicles with high hoods and heavy fenders. He'd whittled axles and wheels, and fashioned tires from shreds of old plastic sandals. With a bit of string tied to the grill and a little pole hooked to the string, he'd towed his automobiles along the rutted unpaved streets of Koidu, a mining town out east.

His father, a part-time tailor, had spent the rest of his time digging for diamonds in the haphazard pits at the edge of town, the moonscape of craters hacked and shoveled and occasionally bulldozed from the jungle, in those years before the last few bulldozers were destroyed by the rebels and the era of machinery reached an end and the mining became, near the turn of the twenty-first century, an enterprise done entirely by hand. But Komba's father had never worked with anything besides a pick and a shovel and a sifter. He was like uncountable thousands of others, pouring sweat all day and standing thigh-deep in pools of parasite-infested khaki-colored water and dreaming that the next batch of gravel they chopped from the pit wall would contain a stone, a gem that would then belong to whoever—a Sierra Leonean, a Gambian, a Lebanese—had supplied the digger's tools, but one that would bring the digger a better payday than the bowl of rice he otherwise worked for. And like uncountable thousands of others, Komba's father had few such paydays.

His death from disease left his family penniless, and for a while Komba went to live with his older sister, hoping she would pay for him to begin school. She could barely support her own kids with the profits she made selling cigarettes on the side of the road. So, never having been inside a classroom, never having known his own age or what year it was by the calendar, Komba returned to his mother's hut and started milling around a local garage.

He was probably around eleven, but so poorly fed he looked younger. The mechanic began to worry that the runtish boy with the broad face and high jutting cheekbones and skinny eyes had been sent by an older gang to case the yard for robbery. He demanded to know what the child was doing. Komba couldn't answer. He was too frightened by the man, too awestruck by the engines. Even when he got hold of himself, he was too desperate with dreams to voice them in public. He stood on tiptoes and the bossman leaned down and he whispered what he wanted into the mechanic's ear. He became the smallest apprentice at the garage, so scrawny he couldn't loosen a bolt no matter how much he heaved and kicked at the wrench.

He was relegated, at first, to wiping down parts. After a few months he could work on valves and plugs. And after a few more months he and his mother and most everyone else fled a rebel attack on the town. The R.U.F. overwhelmed the village they ran to, dug a bayonet into Komba's cheek, took him one way and his gray-haired mother, whom he never saw again, somewhere else. The rebel commander, with unusual modesty, went by his own name of Christopher (not Superman or Rambo or Colonel Savage, as other officers did). And Christopher bandaged the boy's wound (which left a scar like a minor ravine), made him a member of his Termite Squad (named for non-stop destruction), designated Komba the special carrier of his satchel, and thus took over, from the mechanic, as the closest thing Komba had to a father. When he saw that Komba was too weak to carry an AK over long distances, he gave the child a handgun, a Beretta. When Komba had yet to shoot his first man, Christopher ordered his boys to tie and hold a captive, and told Komba to execute him. And after Komba's first battle, during which he mostly hid, Christopher stripped the corpse of a government fighter and handed Komba a uniform. It fit like a clown suit. But "eeeehh," Komba recalled, smiling, "I feel fine." He was now, he explained with proud memories, a soldier.

Christopher taught him how to tie someone "FM," the elbows behind the back so when the rope was cinched and the elbows connected, hard, the person sang in pain. In this way, he bound Komba before flogging him for falling asleep on his watch. He taught the boy how to destroy villages on missions of "food-finding," the all-purpose phrase for all types of raids and pillaging. He fed him before such missions with tabs of unknown pharmaceuticals and cocaine sprinkled into incisions sliced into his shoulders. After battles, he fed him soups thickened with enemy organs. And he took Komba and the rest of the Termite Squad to see the great father, Papa Sankoh, who spoke in the jungle to an assembly of soldiers, spoke of a new Sierra Leone where poverty would be banished and school would be free and, this high among the promises, where every young boy would learn proper English. Then he led the troops in the R.U.F.'s national anthem, written and sung not in Krio nor in any tribal language but with English lyrics the uneducated soldiers knew by heart:

> Go and tell the President, Sierra Leone is my home
> Go and tell my parents, they may see me no more
> When fighting in the battlefield I'm fighting forever
> Every Sierra Leonean is fighting for his land
>
> Sierra Leone is ready to utilize her own
> All our minerals will be accounted for
> The people will enjoy in their land
> R.U.F. is the savior we need right now

Go and tell the President, Sierra Leone is my home
Go and tell my parents, they may see me no more
When fighting in the battlefield I'm fighting forever
Every Sierra Leonean is fighting for his land

R.U.F. is fighting to save Sierra Leone
R.U.F. is fighting to save our people
R.U.F. is fighting to save our country
R.U.F. is fighting to save Sierra Leone

Sankoh's vision, to Komba, was glorious. But when he was probably around fifteen, when his body was starting to fill out with slender muscles and when his cheekbones began to be padded by a bit of flesh, he lashed out against Christopher and left the R.U.F. It happened because of a girl Komba found while food-finding, a pretty girl he seized behind a house where she'd been hiding. He presented her as a gift to his commander, who claimed her in the basic ceremony of wartime marriage, which was rape. Then, because she was very pretty, Christopher made her his head of household, his "mammy queen," and Komba, who was still quite short, found himself treated as a child, humiliated by the girl he had captured. She ordered him to help cook, to fetch water, indignities he had grown beyond, and when he refused, and when Christopher tried to flog him, he fought back, managed to run. He wound up with the West Side Boys, a militia formed of government troops and whoever else clung on. It specialized in ambushing buses along the main road an hour east of Freetown. And soon Komba was head of his own small crew, a father-figure in his own right.

It was a phase without much fighting around that stretch of pavement, and he and his boys could raid and rob at will, then trade with the Nigerian troops who were, at that point, manning roadblocks as members of a West African peacekeeping force, just as they would soon man them for the U.N. But a dispute over business, over a looted camera Komba had given a peacekeeper to sell, led to his youngest soldier getting stabbed to death on the road. Komba caught the Nigerian who did it, bound him FM, and brought him back to his base.

His revenge on the peacekeeper he recounted one evening in my hotel bungalow in Freetown. Komba was a teenager who favored a pair of fashionably baggy athletic shorts with blue soccer balls down the sides. A pattern of thumbtack-sized scars covered his back from neck to waist. The design was composed of inverted Vs bisected by a double line along the spine, a geometry whose meaning and power he would not reveal. He was a boy who had smiled when I'd fallen into teaching him what his childhood hadn't included, the sounds of the alphabet, and when he had managed to print his first name.

"I chook em," he said. At my hotel, the modern world surrounded us, to a degree. The air conditioner was rattling away with the grinding of the hotel's generator. There was an intermittently working phone up the path at the front desk and a TV playing CNN at the open-air bar. Down the road was a disco booming a sweet-voiced ballad above a reverberating bass line, and up the hill overlooking the sea the Chinese were slowly building a resort hotel of unadorned concrete, in case peace ever came and tourists returned to the beaches. There were cell phones and of course there was traffic, and many Sierra Leoneans were listening to the BBC on their transistor radios and were far better informed on international affairs than my countrymen back home.

"I chook em," he said as he described—in Krio, in perfectly straightforward tones—how his boys had held the peacekeeper on the ground, how he'd rammed his bayonet into the base of the man's throat, and how he'd yanked the blade downward across the body, ripping open the chest and belly. "For me bobo he wen kill, I killah, pull de livah. I take de dead livah, de heart. I boilah. Chop dat," he said, using the Krio word for eat, and next a word for malign willfulness: *mind.* " 'You have mind,' " he recalled holding the liver over the man's face. " 'This your mind.' " Then he spoke partly in English, emphasizing his reasons—not only the fatal stabbing of his boy but the Nigerian's dishonest dealings—before he summarized why the man's punishment had been necessary:

"He make I feel bad."

I asked Komba, another evening, for more explanation, not of that one incident but, in general, of the eating of organs and drinking of blood he and other soldiers carried out against their enemies. Was it part of any ritual, a way to acquire power? He said it was not, that no ceremony was attached to it, no significance beyond retribution.

There were other explanations, of course. Some in the community of foreign aid workers and human rights advocates argued that the practice was pushed on kidnapped soldiers as a way to isolate them permanently from civilian society and bind them to their commanders. Others said it was simply a way to terrify everyone, to secure the nation's acquiescence, so that men like Foday Sankoh could rule as they wished. And from a kidnapped woman I heard of ritual aspects, not in the way of cannibalism but of sacrifice: a calabash filled with the blood of slaughtered children, and fighters touching the blood for protection before heading off on attack.

Whatever the reasons, civil war had stirred the forces of atavism. Old cannibalistic and sacrificial rites (which, I was told by any number of Sierra Leoneans, elite and uneducated alike, were still sometimes enacted beyond the scope of the war by the country's traditional juju men) had flourished in new, anarchic forms within the fighting.

It was fighting that Komba now meant to leave behind. At a U.N. demobilization camp—a sun-assaulted field, a cyclone-fenced holding pen with long tents and packs of teenagers alternately stupefied and enraged to find themselves without their weapons—he had turned in his rifle. The decision to do this had not been his own. One of the top commanders in the West Side Boys, making a gesture of peace, a play for government power before he returned to warfare, had ordered Komba to surrender with his unit. And Komba had let go of his gun in fear. What else did he know as well as violence? For the past five years, what other means of subsistence had he had? But gradually over the coming months he had resolved to attempt a new life, to find work in a capital without jobs, to create a future that had nothing to do with being a soldier—to become, as he'd long ago dreamed, an auto mechanic—while, all around him, the war sucked his country back into the past.

FIVE From his helicopter, Neall Ellis dropped government leaflets over rebel-held towns. The message on one sheet was laid out around a picture of his huge, camouflage-patterned MI-24 helicopter gunship:

> **RUF:**
> **this time we've**
> **dropped leaflets**
> **Next time it will be:**
> **a half inch Gatling machine gun or**
> **57mm rockets or**
> **23mm guns or**
> **30mm grenades or**
> **ALL OF THEM!**

Another sheet took a different tone:

> **We've all been friends**
> **We can be friends again . . .**
> **Join us in the**
> **new Sierra Leone**

These six- by eight-inch slips of paper floated down over markets. And soon after—within minutes, townspeople said—Neall returned to unload his arsenal at several enemy vehicles, parked by the market squares. The areas were crowded. A few of the vehicles, Neall said, were trucks with mounted machine guns. "I'm sorry, of course I'm sorry, I don't want to kill civilians. But I'm not going to lose sleep over it, because I can't. There's been a lot of people killed. I cannot run my life based on looking back at

how many civilians have been killed by accident. I won't be effective. And the fact is that when people hear that helicopter
coming, they mustn't just stand around and watch, if they are
innocent."

His Gatling gun fired about eighty thick bullets per second.
His rockets sent shrapnel everywhere. Human Rights Watch reported twenty-seven civilian dead and fifty wounded in attacks
on three towns. People told of a baby killed, a pregnant woman
ripped apart. Some had just rushed out to collect the leaflets.

Neall belonged to what others in the field sometimes called
the world's second oldest profession. He was a mercenary soldier. He was white, had grown up in Rhodesia, and trained in
South Africa. A veteran of the war to save white dominion, he
was now employed by Kabbah's government and overseen by the
British who ran what Kabbah had of a military. He loved his
work, the risk, the gamble. "It's a game, war," he said. Fifty years
old, he stood around five feet eight inches tall, with a sharp nose
and a soft middle. "It's the biggest and best game in the history
of mankind."

I'd first met him in a waterside Freetown bar called Paddy's
Chinese Restaurant. Vast though it was, with room to park a fleet
of helicopters, on weekends you couldn't turn a shoulder amidst
the aid workers and the diamond dealers, the British officers
and the gun merchants and the U.N. accountants, the all-
purpose businessmen in timber export or cell phone tower
construction or whatever else came along, and the security en-
trepreneurs, former mercenaries themselves, who thrived, supplying private armed guards to relief groups in the frontier
atmosphere of Sierra Leone.

The place was filled, too, with girls. Paddy, an elderly and
longtime British fixture in the capital, had recently received, at
Buckingham Palace, an M.B.E. from the Queen, a medal honor-

ing him as a Member of the British Empire. It was, people said, for providing prostitutes to any Englishman who washed up on this shore, but Paddy, tall and angular, eyes always smiling graciously behind thick glasses, seemed befuddled by the hangarsized saloon that had grown up around him. He played bridge off in a corner and liked to tell the story of his ten seconds with her majesty: "And what do you do in Sierra Leone?" she asked when he reached the head of the line of honorees. "I run a bar, ma'am." "Oh," the queen said, a bit startled, "a bar." And meanwhile the girls glittered in their high-gloss makeup and highgloss spandex. The shine betrayed no disintegration beneath. There was nothing used up about them. They were too young for that.

Nor were they exactly prostitutes, not most of them, not in the set-fee-for-specific-act sense of the word. Things were subtler than that, more flattering and less expensive for the men. The girls were hoping for a free dinner, for a small, unnegotiated "gift" of money to pass along to their parents, for—if they were extremely lucky—the status symbol of a cell phone that might come from a long-term relationship. It sometimes seemed that here at Paddy's, far more than in any work of rescue, the meeting of disparate worlds, Western and African, white and black, reached its full expression. The night I met Neall, there was a caramel-colored girl, half-Lebanese and half-African, whose tank top had a teardrop-shaped peekaboo hole between her breasts, another with a face like a young Janet Jackson, one around thirteen whose hips were as razor straight as her ass was round, another whose floral skirt flounced at the top of her powerful, very dark thighs. "There's the social life you wouldn't get anywhere else," a British businessman had told me, when I'd asked why he chose to live so far from home. It was clear what he meant, but his tone wasn't cynical or leering, only frank. Well into middleage, of middling looks and making no Western-scale fortune, where else could he be so satisfied, so prized? Where else could he have the devotion of teenage girlfriends as well as the solace of a beautiful Sierra Leonean wife who couldn't have been much older than thirty?

It didn't seem to bother the men that many of the girls had their clitorises cut, the pervasive custom in Sierra Leone. Perhaps it was considered a plus. Nor did AIDS seem to slow anyone down. "The Great Loorgi," Neall called the disease, and though I could never figure out the etymology, the name somehow captured the general attitude about the illness, that it was both a plague and a joke. There was no way of knowing the nation's infection rate, but given the polygamous culture and the omnipresence of soldiers (not only Sierra Leoneans but U.N. troops from all over Africa), and given the war's rampant sexual violence, the rate was sure to be high. (Among the girls who were regulars at places like Paddy's, the World Health Organization had managed an estimate back in 1995. Even then, the rate had already been more than one in four.) Yet without anything resembling a public health care system to educate the population, Sierra Leoneans seemed largely doubtful about the cause of the sickness, with the men tending toward "flavor" over protection. Meanwhile the expats put on their condoms and crossed their fingers.

But that night Neall wasn't distracted by the pointed sidelong looks the girls gave as they wedged past. He was more compelled by something else. "Look," he said, "you get the cliché, Better than sex. But you're taking fire. There's a lot of adrenaline going. You're all keyed up, and when you realize you're on target, that you've taken out the enemy, it's a great feeling, it's a great relief." Back from his missions, home in bed, he fell asleep like a man whose spectacular orgasm has blasted him into a night's unconsciousness, fell fast and deep, "because you have that adrenaline high, and you're exhausted, mentally, it's so stimulating, that adrenaline, I suppose it's like a drug . . ."

I asked about the rumor that the rebels had mercenaries of their own, Ukrainians or former colleagues of Neall's from

South Africa, training them to be better shots with their anti-aircraft guns. I thought it made his income, $6,000 a month, seem somewhat small.

"The only way to confirm it is by helicopter," he answered, meaning by his being shot down. He smiled in his minimal way, lips hardly moving, barely acknowledging his sly joke.

The speakers blared "My Eyes Adored You," a hit from my homeland, from decades ago. In the far reaches of the bar, folding chairs had been set up and a beauty contest was underway, not a joke competition for near-hookers but, apparently, a sincere civic event, judged by Sierra Leonean dignitaries, men in suits and women in gowns. In a war zone like this, a place like Paddy's was where beauty queens were crowned.

"You working tomorrow?" a man asked, shifting by, wondering casually if Neall was taking Sunday off.

"Yes," the mercenary said, soft denim shirt tucked loosely into khakis.

"When will you be finished?"

"Hope to get done early. Around three."

Then, voice changing abruptly, he turned back to me. "I hate the R.U.F. When you see what they've done to these people, to this country. Sometimes I get too emotional. You go to the amputee camps and see."

He held my gaze, his brown eyes made powerful by his falcon-like nose. He wasn't going to say more. Emotions weren't supposed to enter into it.

He sipped his beer, spoke about the British. They were committed, he said, and well meaning, but there was no way they could succeed. "This war's going to be going on two, four, ten years from now."

I wanted to ask if that was a sad prediction or a personal wish, given the work he needed for a good night's sleep, but we'd been getting interrupted, and now, as the city's eleven o'clock curfew came near, the interruptions increased. Time was running out. People wanted money. A woman needed school

fees for her son. Another needed medicine. They didn't go to
the businessmen and British majors and aid workers around
us. They didn't ask me. Five, six, seven, eight people in an hour,
they pushed and weaved their way toward Neall, appeared at his
side. He knew most by name. He reached into the breast pocket
of his pale blue shirt and, with no sign of annoyance, gave out
the equivalent of two or five or, to a second mother looking for a
child's tuition, forty dollars. It turned out he was paying, too, for
a young man to go to medical school.

   "I'm getting old," Neall said, preferring to explain his char-
ity as sheer self-interest. "I'm going to want a doctor."

He was the most famous expatriate in Sierra Leone. In the diamond pits out past Bo, the diggers stripped to their blue and
green briefs knew him simply as "the Pilot." Along the jungle
tracks, in the silver gauze of rainy season sunlight, the children
hauling jerricans of red palm oil for cooking, heading to town
markets twenty miles away with eighty-pound loads dangling
from poles across their shoulders, called him "the South
African." Over the past couple of years, his helicopter had
seemed the only thing keeping the rebels and government army
mutineers from overruning every pit and grove.

   And at the abandoned hotel where Komba had been
shipped after the demobilization camp, a hotel where two priests
and a nun hoped to coax boys like him, and boys half as old,
away from their brutal histories, on a wall by the ocean the ex-
soldiers had painted a mural. There was a big yellow chicken saying "bye bye war" in a bubble popping from its beak. There were
little green huts and a lollipop-shaped tree and, looming over it,
a helicopter gunship, the only weapon shown. The Nigerian
bomber jets were nothing, the kids said. The gunship was very
bad. You couldn't see or hear it coming till it was too late to run.
You could shoot at it "to tension it," but you couldn't bring it
down. From a gunship barrage, one of the kids was missing half

his leg. And next to the helicopter in the mural flew a yellow butterfly, as childishly rendered as the lollipop tree, wings six times
the size of the gunship's blades.

"I don't like sort of boasting or anything like that," Neall
said, "but I'm prepared to say that if it wasn't for myself and my
team you wouldn't be here today. Or you would be here under
very different circumstances." In 1998, again in 1999, and just recently in the spring of 2000, he felt he'd rescued the faint hope
of democracy with his resupplying of trapped defenders and
shuttling of hunting society militiamen into battle zones—and
with his lone assaults on advancing R.U.F. And it would have
sounded like boasting, except that I kept hearing other people
give him the same credit. "He's a bit of a nutter," Captain Smith,
the British spokesman, said, about Neall's stunts in 2000, before the British got their commandos fully established on the
ground: his attempts to draw fire as a way to locate and destroy
enemy artillery, his all but suicidal methods of slowing the attack
on the capital. "But he single-handedly saved Freetown."

He'd learned to fly in Mozambique and Rhodesia, South
West Africa and Angola, in the wars South Africa waged to keep
the threat against apartheid from creeping too close. "Shit, this
is pretty good fun," he recalled his feelings after the first time he
was shot at, the rounds zipping through the helicopter between
the back of his head and the troops he was flying into position.
His voice didn't rise with the memory; his tone stayed tight. "It
just seemed a very exciting experience. And the second time,
this was up in Angola, a cas-evac mission, all of a sudden I hear
this ticking noise. This typewriter noise." A 12.7 millimeter machine gun was taking aim from down below. " 'Pull away, pull
away, back off, fuck off,' " one of the crew yelled. Sent to evacu-
ate wounded in a helicopter not rigged for firepower, they had
only a shotgun on board. Neall told him to try it. " 'I'm going to
pop over this church so you can shoot the guy,' " he remembered. "The next moment I had the shotgun put to my head,
and he said, 'Listen, Lieutenant, I think we should fuck off.' "

And boasting might have seemed the least of it—might have seemed to slide into a soldier's fabrications, especially since I had no way to confirm this story—but for the constant restraint of his voice and the kamikaze portrait everyone else rendered.

"I was shitting in my pants," a British sergeant described what was supposed to be a routine transit flight he'd just taken, 250 kilometers per hour at an altitude no higher than the nearest grass roof.

"Were you flying with Ellis?" I asked.

"I flew," he said, "with a crazy South African bastard."

Neall's politics, in South Africa, had been as hard-core as his ways of flying. Afrikaner on his mother's side, British on his father's, he "dabbled on the fringes," he told me, of the terrorist Afrikaner Resistance Movement, and joined the American-based Church of the Creator, whose doctrine read: "A creator recognizes both love and hate as the two most powerful driving forces in life: that both emotions are healthy and essential . . . He loves, aids, and abets those of his own race and his own kind, and hates his enemies, namely Jews, niggers, and the mud races."

Yet there had been contradictions: a long affair with a woman of mixed race; the slow realization, within a white society he described as cut off from the movements of the world, that "she's a normal human being like you," that "our blood is red and everything beneath is pink and everybody's got feelings"; the thought that the apartheid regime was "more aligned to Hitler's way of thinking than to a normal human being's way of thinking."

Still, "it was just a question of existence. We were the whites of South Africa. We had a right to live there, I was born there, so it's my country. And if you looked at the rest of Africa, the winds of change sweeping through Africa, what had happened to the white settlers and the white businesspeople—I saw what happened in Rhodesia. And I start realizing I've got nowhere to go. I've got no money. I've got no great qualifications. And all those Rhodesians and Mozambiquans, the white Portuguese, they could emigrate south. But when you get to South Africa you go as far as Capetown and there's nowhere to go. I didn't know what to do. It was a question of if I would survive in South Africa, if I would fight or if I would go down. So I fought."

But when the white government started to give up on apartheid around 1990, his superiors saw him as a white warrior-fanatic, incapable of giving up his battle. They began to ease him out.

"I'm not making excuses. I'm not apologizing for anyone. I'm not apologizing for myself. Right now I see there were a lot of wrongs that were done. The concept of apartheid was wrong. But at one time I thought it was the only way forward. There was nowhere else to go."

And in the end, the nowhere he'd wound up in was Sierra Leone. He said he was happy here, that he was going to settle here, that "the least I can do is contribute on the military side." He said, "I'm going to die here." He gave only a hint of his minimal smile, and his steady eyes revealed nothing. I couldn't tell what he saw behind them: a vision, past the war, of a death in old age; or a vision of falling, of fireballs and explosion.

The medical student he was supporting came by one morning after Neall and I had breakfast. Neall had hosted. With his Sierra Leonean girlfriend leaning against his porch rail, Neall had spread a yellow-and-white tablecloth over a makeshift table fashioned from a sheet of steel. He set out matching plates and glasses, utensils wrapped delicately within napkins, a graceful pitcher of juice. The woman, motionless in blue chiffon and black lingerie, was stunning enough to make any man rethink his life's priorities, and that morning, despite or because of her presence, and the existence of his other Sierra Leonean lover, his "sympathy wife," in England where he was putting her through nursing and midwifery school, and his legal wife long behind in South Africa, and the attentions of the Freetown girls he met in the bars, Neall seemed utterly lost and, in his reserved way, desperate to make some kind of connection that went beyond whatever he had with the woman at the rail, who kept her back turned, who said nothing, whose blue chiffon I tried not to stare at and through.

He emerged again from the kitchen with the impeccably shaped mushroom omelet he'd cooked. He cut the omelet into perfect slices. Then he plated: the lightly and evenly browned eggs, yellow corn, red beans, hues all complementing. "I suppose I went too far with the pepper," he said as we began to eat, said it tersely but anxiously, searching for reassurance, fishing for praise.

His big, stark house was behind a sandbagged guard post in a camp of U.N. soldiers. From the porch, the view started with the rag curtains of the peacekeepers' latrine. The bizarre bombed-out edifice of the government's defense headquarters—like the ruins of some enormous Martian spaceship—lay at the base of the hill, with Neall's helipad to one side. But if you looked beyond that you saw the lagoon, the entire expanse of it, the untroubled water spreading inward from the sea like a balm. And then there was the sea itself, and the fishermen's long, low, untroubled canoes.

"I love this country," Neall said. "This is home."

Maybe I was wrong. Maybe Neall wasn't lost at all. Maybe this war zone, horrid and beautiful, *was* home. And maybe somehow, with the woman who drifted silently away from the rail and into the house, not invited to join us and probably not interested in doing so, there was a real connection, a bond at a depth I couldn't perceive and forged from things I was incapable of understanding. Later, as Neall and I walked through the house, past the few pieces of furniture and African art, we came upon the woman sitting with a group of friends in the air-conditioned living room.

"The black people are supposed to be outside in the heat," Neall said, gesturing toward the porch.

"Then the white people," the woman said sharply, "should not sit where the black should be."

We all laughed, Neall not in his usual compressed way. It wasn't much, but it was, in all my time in Sierra Leone, one of the few moments when I witnessed something like easy friendship between a white expatriate and a Sierra Leonean, and when I felt that race had been somewhat transcended.

Then we returned to the porch, and soon the medical student arrived, for tuition, rent money, living expenses. "Father," Michael Josiah called Neall quietly, and all the hierarchies were back in the air.

He wore a new safari vest, pressed jeans, tan hiking boots. His closely shaved head was narrow, his face thin, his nose and lips faintly Semitic. His body was almost wispy, but his presence —inward, nimble—was poised in a way that made his skinniness irrelevant; he occupied space with an aura of calm self-certainty. "Father," he said, deferent and even fearful in the way of complete dependence. But he wasn't groveling.

Michael, who had grown up partly in the capital, partly up-country, had spent his young childhood dissecting frogs. He would catch the frogs himself, slit them open with a razor blade. "I would examine all the entrails, the tubing of the intestines. I would examine the digested matter, and after, I would put the tubes back inside. Then I would take a needle and thread and stitch the frog back up. But oh, when my father caught me . . . " Michael laughed at the memory. "He would cane me for a wicked boy."

It had gone on for years, the slicing and sewing and caning, though Michael knew the innards by heart, until at last he had lost interest, devoted himself to soccer. But he had wound up studying medicine at what was left of the national university, its original colonial building a refugee camp, its newer concrete blocks, surrounded by shrubs in fabulous bloom, holding classrooms filled with broken chairs and bathrooms without running water.

He left almost as soon as he'd begun. Kabbah had been overthrown, and Michael joined the Civil Defense Forces, the coalition of tribal hunting societies—Gbenties from the Temne people of the north; Kamajors from Michael's tribe, the Mende of the south and east—that had gone to war, at first, to protect their own territories from the rebels. As the war intensified, the societies initiated thousands to fight with them, and Michael, enraged by the coup, became a C.D.F. soldier to restore the democracy that had lasted barely a year. "The junta was something like a cancer," he remembered thinking, when I asked if he'd hesitated before leaving his studies, when I asked if he'd been afraid. "Of course I was, initially, a bit. In fact, I will tell you, perhaps more than a bit. In fact, after my first battle, I went two or three days with my arms aching, my muscles had been so contracted, holding the gun so tightly. But if you leave this cancer the patient is going to die. You have no choice but to remove it."

And then his father, who had worked as a radio operator for the national mining company, back when there had been a national mining company, and later as a small-time prospector on his own, died of tuberculosis. Michael's chances for more schooling collapsed. He had little money and brothers and sisters to take care of. But he'd gotten to know Neall at the C.D.F. base where the pilot loaded Kamajor initiates to fly into position. Neall had told him he could count on full support.

Ever since, with Kabbah restored, Michael had alternated between fighting (whenever the opposition seemed close to victory) and medical school. During the Freetown invasion that cost Lamin his hands, he had battled to push the insurgents away from the capital. When the enemy was twenty-five miles outside, school reopened and Michael returned to his books. This was how normal war had become in Sierra Leone, and how focused Michael could be. With the most brutal soldiers in the world twenty-five miles away, he crammed over biochemistry and hematology.

Now, from the porch, Neall had wandered off to do some of-

fice work inside or to check a mercenary list-serve on-line, and
Michael and I went on talking: about Freetown's hospital, its
doctors making seventy dollars per month, and about the future.
"To turn this country around, oh, the strength must be Herculean." Our conversation snagged. His accent was slight, and
the flourishes in his speech were unforced, but I hadn't understood "Herculean." He repeated it several times; somehow my
mind couldn't get it.

"I don't know the word," I said. "I'm sorry. I'm sure you're
right."

He unzipped a small bag, pulled out a tattered paperback
dictionary, flipped at high speed through the pages, and four
seconds later held the book toward me. He pointed with his elegant finger to prove himself right.

Between microbiology and physiology and dissecting corpses
in anatomy ("You can never know what is in the living," he said,
"without knowing exactly what is in the dead"), he wore, in battle, a belt filled with substances he did not know. It was a simple
belt, two strips of stitched leather, bought in the market. Following C.D.F. tradition, he'd taken it to a Kamajor high priest, who,
overnight, broke the stitching, inserted the substances, resewed
the leather, and blessed the result. In combat, the belt had saved
him more than once. It had tightened hard around his waist to
warn him of ambush. It had diverted bullets. "Initially," he said,
"I was shocked to see what I have seen. And even when I *had*
seen it, still I was skeptical. Only over time I trusted." When bullets hit him, he "experienced a sharp impact. But there was nothing. No skin abrasion, not even that. Simply that the material of
my jeans jacket was burned in that area."

He had to take care with the belt when he wasn't fighting,
though. If his new wife mistakenly came upon it, if she touched
it, she would be barren . . .

. . . I had been invited, one afternoon, to a display of power
by a hunting society priest, a Gbentie named Commander
Snake. I'd met him while out with a British patrol that was gath-

ering intelligence, getting to know the terrain, the proximity of enemy troops. Layers of white cowries and red pompons and black yarn burgeoned from his headdress. Woven amulets in turquoise and red and royal blue studded his old sweater vest. He carried a whisk of black and white monkey hair. He wore ropes of braided orange, a necklace with a mirrored pendant, wraparound sunglasses that were slightly bent, and a narrow line of beard, perfectly straight, running from the precise center of his lower lip to the midpoint of his chin. In front of his jungle headquarters, a colonial ruin with carved sills and a portico with an ornate rail, he stood with a slender tan-patterned viper slipping between the fingers of each hand. Another writhed and coiled in the air, head in the priest's mouth.

Manning his roadblock—a bit of string across the mud track—a cluster of boys, unadorned, held rusty twin-barreled shotguns or AKs with stickers from karate films. The British had brought along a local translator, and through him the priest said he'd taken most of his weapons in fighting against the R.U.F. or, lately, the West Side Boys. "No enemy," he declared, "will remove me." The snakes would never bite him because of his power. Artillery could not strike him, could not even fire in his direction, because of his whisk. The rounds would fly back toward the one who had shot them. Sometimes, he explained, he fought naked except for a headpiece. He offered the British a demonstration of his immunity to bullets.

The U.K. soldiers took quick glances at one another. They laughed from the restraint of desire. To say yes would have been far outside their rules—and I was there. So everyone shook hands (one British forearm bore a tattooed skull surrounded by flames and crowned by a dagger), and the two British Land Rovers, one with a heavy machine gun, started up. But I, along for the ride, wasn't under any rules. If I found my way back to this spot the next day, I asked Snake, would he put on his demonstration?

He stripped down to burlap pants the following afternoon.

He wasn't tall, and his slim body was lightly muscled; half-naked, standing on ground dotted with tiny yellow bell flowers and surrounded by trees with leaves the size of dinner plates, he looked too fragile even to claim any particular strength, let alone possess it. And he wasn't saying anything as he prepared himself, bending over a brown liquid in a white enamel bowl.

He dabbed the substance on his bare shoulders. Liquids like this, their ingredients known only to spiritual leaders like Snake, had played a major part in the war. Whatever their effect on bullets, they had inspired thousands of initiates to fight, often triumphantly, against the R.U.F. and its allies. And the enemy, it was said, sometimes ran without fighting, knowing their weapons to be useless against such inoculation.

Keeping his narrow back to the crowd of fifty, the remaining population of the war-razed settlement, Snake now misted his chest and belly with the contents of a perfume bottle. Then he took up an old mustard bottle with a squirt tip. Everyone was hushed. His movements more dutiful than grand or dramatic, he slathered on more of the watery brown mixture, coated his arms and ribs and nipples and neck. And he turned to face us.

He had already positioned a thirteen- or fourteen-year-old soldier forty feet away, and the boy lifted his assault rifle. The crowd went audibly taut. People shifted without moving, were loud without speaking. The boy hoisted the gun to his shoulder. Snake waited—calm, still, unrigid—for the gun to go off. The boy aimed. The noise of the blast was stunning. The commander buckled, winced, grabbed his belly, started to pull. He tugged a bullet from a small fold in his gut. The crowd cheered, seemed relieved but not much surprised. Did they truly believe? I couldn't tell. And maybe they saw as I was incapable of seeing, knew something I was incapable of knowing, that what had seemed the equivalent of a carnival trick hadn't been a trick at all.

A truckload of government soldiers—uniformed, helmeted, newly graduated from a British course like Captain Rosenfeld's—happened to have driven by near the end of Snake's display. After the boy had taken his shot, they wanted a turn. Snake agreed. He asked someone to bring his sacred vest, its square charms "filled"—he would reveal nothing more specific—"with good things." He draped it over a wooden pole, painted it with the fluids in the bowl, the perfume bottle, the mustard container. He stepped away, offering only the garment.

The British-trained soldiers didn't argue or joke about the change of target. It wasn't at all clear that they thought Snake's power a scam. (Throughout the war, plenty of government troops, among them Mike Kpukumu, Strasser's security chief, had arranged to go through hunting society immunizations.) The soldiers seemed only to want a part in the event, and the vest seemed no less significant than the priest's body.

A helmeted gunman went down on one knee. He fired six times. Everyone ran to the target, counted six jagged exit wounds ripped out the back of the wool. The uniformed soldiers were gone before I could ask how they explained it. But Snake said he had let too many women too near the vest. It had been "spoiled," weakened, its spiritual purity breached. There was a similar reason for any inoculated man being killed or wounded in combat. It might not be women. It might be something else. But always he had weakened his protection by breaking the spiritual laws . . .

. . . As he spoke of the belt, Michael wanted to make something understood. He had "reservations, religious reservations" about such powers. "I know that the powers work, but I am a Christian. I am civilized. There are only two forces in the world, and this kind of thing can only come from one. I want to be civilized." So while he talked of the things he had experienced, and the miracles he had seen "as clearly as bacteria under the microscope," an undertone of shame lingered beneath the open pride he took in what his nation's traditional priests could accomplish and the excitement he felt in his plans.

He would finish medical school, he said, and then, "after, I will establish a research laboratory." He would analyze the traditional substances. He would convince the priests to let their exact leaf and bark ingredients be known. "Your name," he would tell them, "your contribution to the science of medicine, will surely have its record." Then he would run clinical trials and publish papers in Western journals. He would prove that the mixtures could cure incurable diseases. People would flock to Sierra Leone. Because though the papers would list the elements of the medicines and demonstrate the value of the treatments, they would not reveal an essential part in the preparation of the substances: the blessings of the priests. Michael would never ask for those, not even for himself. So the world would have to reach Sierra Leone in order to be healed.

And it was possible to entertain—regardless of the blessings—part of Michael's desire. Maybe, in his search for medical breakthroughs, he would find some spectacular cure in the nation's plant life, and maybe, if he handled his discovery in just the right way, it would save his country from becoming a netherworld.

I asked how he reconciled traditional and Western systems of knowledge, suggested that a Western doctor might say he had to give up the first to be a doctor at all.

"Life is complex. You don't have to be dogmatic. Think beyond the normal. Certain people think that red is red, it can never be green. But you look beyond that. If someone says red is green, look beyond—there must be something reflecting that is green. I do believe that if I can bring modern medicine together with the traditional powers, what I have studied up to this point with what I have seen, when I have put those two things together I can manage great exploits. I can contribute to the development of mankind."

SIX Lilies surfaced in the swamps. White moonflowers opened at dusk. Among the blossoms, long before the war, Mary Kortenhoven took refuge. The flame trees bloomed red and the camel's foot sprang purple and the loofah erupted in spongy fruit. Glorioso spread their vines, triplets of flowers flushing from yellow to rich orange. Children brought her purple orchids, scarcely an inch high. The frangipani and gardenias and birds of paradise she planted around the house grew ecstatically, all brilliant petals and high-gloss leaves. With a stick she knocked grapefruit from branches. The rain fell like curtains of glass beads. Bananas dangled from green awnings and pineapples lolled under spiky crowns. The path to the waterfall led through walls vivid as jewels.

The refuge she needed was from disease, from the village women who stood with hands on heads in the Kuronko posture of bereavement, from their wailing—the shrill quavering note continuing on and on, interrupted only for breath, announcing that a son or daughter had died or answering in a chorus of mourning. When the measles arrived in 1983, the single note played relentlessly, filling the atmosphere Mary walked through. She needed to treat the children of Foria, the kids in all the villages covered by the family's mission. She had to reach those other places before the epidemic raged completely, before it did what it had in Yara, a settlement of thirty mud huts and twenty-three new deaths. There the village chief lost all five of his children. To make it to those places she had to cross the vine-strung suspension bridges, twenty-five feet in the air, that looked, to her, skinny as tightropes. Their palm siding looked flimsy as paper. Terrified, she could not force herself to walk. Her few medical supplies in her backpack, she crossed on her knees.

She was not propelled by fanatic devotion. She was a quiet woman in a long checked skirt and gray ruffled blouse who would rather have been tending flowers, a woman who kept with her in Africa stacks of home decorating magazines, and who might, in another life, have been a collector of country antiques. This life she had fallen into. There had been no missionaries in her family of successful Ohio farmers, producers of celery and lettuce and radishes. And there had been no moment of calling.

Before Foria, she and Paul had been on two African missions, in the late '60s and early '70s, both times to far less remote postings in Nigeria. The first trip had happened almost by chance. Shortly before they were married, Paul had been teaching seventh-grade English, history, and math in a public school in Chicago, and thinking of graduate school in psychology or law. One day over lunch, Mary, a senior at the Christian Reformed Church's Calvin College in Grand Rapids, had mentioned—flippantly—hearing of a need for teachers in Nigeria. Maybe, she said, he should try that, since he couldn't figure out anything else. Flippancy had turned to shared imagining. But the imagining had more to do with adventure than faith. For Mary, any faint inclination to proselytize had come down to a private knowledge—"Jesus loves me, this I know"—and the wish to share that comfort. Paul, who had also gone to Calvin, and who sometimes strummed his guitar and sang Christian songs to a gathering of children on his front lawn, was still considering the LSAT. Their first posting was supposed to be a year's diversion before real life began.

Mary's parents had wondered if she could handle even a year. Her voice sometimes shy to the point of being inaudible, she'd seemed almost too timorous to venture from Ohio to Michigan for college. And though she had proven her parents wrong, and had handled that first year in Africa, still she had never taken easily to the communal and public style of African living—she craved, for much of her time in Foria, the pleasure of solitude, of reading a book or merely sitting alone, without the perpetual intrusions and endless lingering of the villagers. There was little chance for privacy. And there was hardly the chance to want it when the epidemics swept through.

The measles brought high fever, and high fever stirred intestinal worms, several inches long, into a tumult. Worms spilled from the children's noses. The insides of their mouths filled with sores. The disease, weakening bodies already chronically weak from the infections the villagers lived with and the poor diets they got by on, opened the way for pneumonia, for meningitis. The children curled torpid on the ground. They died within a few days of their first symptoms. The graves lay directly behind the huts, brief mounds of dirt, a blanket of palm branches. Parents poured kerosene down their children's throats, trying to make the sickness come out before it killed them. Above the village pathways, the people draped string adorned with red rags, to make this devil go away.

Mary listened with her stethoscope to lungs that crackled like cellophane. She was not a nurse, but between the instruction of two of the other missionaries her church had sent into the region and her own obsessive reading, she basically became one. Practicing on oranges, she taught herself to use a hypodermic, so she could inject antibiotics. She taught the Kuronko mothers to mix a rehydration drink—boiled water and salt and sugar and lemon juice. She taught them how crucial it was to spoon the liquid into their children's slack mouths. She tried to convince them that this—and not the kerosene—might save their babies' lives. There was success more than failure. Sometimes a girl like Sera, cured of both measles and whooping cough, came to Mary's door, dressed in her scraps of *lappa*, to thank her. But scores died in Foria, scores more in Sulia and Yisais. Mary hiked to Kwansiokoro, treated about twenty-five, and prayed that these would live. In the settlement's twelve homes, fifteen children were already gone.

During the time of the epidemic, if the wailing ever paused in Foria, she could hear it floating in from the surrounding hills.

And then cholera surged through from Guinea, the body drained of all fluid within hours, the flesh so parched, so raisin-like, that if you pressed the skin it never regained its shape. The villagers died excruciating deaths behind their huts, while she and Paul strung IV tubes—countless plastic vines—from the trees.

This, somehow, was where they belonged. Mary and Paul watched Aaron, their six-year-old son, learn Kuranko with sudden speed after his months of early despair. With his friends he worked in the mud, helping his neighbors to make bricks and to build walls and, if the villager could afford the dung sold by the Fula traders, to spread dung over the exterior, smoothing the hut's façade. Taking a break, a boy named Foray tried to crack everyone up with a universal childhood contortion: flipping his eyelid inside-out. A photograph commemorates the eyelid, the camaraderie, Aaron crusted in muck, his friend Marah with a hand on Aaron's bare shoulder. Once, on a visit back to the States, Aaron showed the picture to his grandfather. "I'm the one in the middle," he said, as though his grandfather might need help in telling the boys apart, as though Aaron had forgotten the straw color of his long, uncombed hair or the color of the fingers resting near his collarbone.

A family story had Aaron leading the Kortenhovens to Sierra Leone in the first place. They'd been living in Minnesota, where Paul, who'd gone to seminary between stints in Nigeria, was minister to a small church. And when he and Mary resolved to take on another mission, they had, in their dining room with its round oak table and three-tiered plant stand, spun the family globe. Aaron had put down his finger—the very first time—on Sierra Leone, and as Sierra Leone was among the countries the Christian Reformed Church had chosen for evangelism and development, Aaron's finger decided everything.

And now he was learning which Kuronkoland fruits to eat,

which plants had edible parts, how to fold two leaves into a cup
to draw water from a thread-thin stream. Mary and Paul would
see him walking through the village in his fringed and pom-
ponned Kuronko cap, chewing kola nuts and carrying a machete.

"Dear Grandma Gene and Grandpa Pete," Aaron wrote the
next year, after a local hunter had given the family a baby chimp
whose mother the hunter had killed. The kids had diapered and
cuddled it, let it nap on their pillows and drink from their cups,
but eventually, led by Matthew in his bowl haircut and knee-high
triple-striped tube socks, they took it back where the hunter had
been. "Once we had a chimpanzee," Aaron dictated the letter to
his mother. "She was funny. If we put her down she would cry.
The chimp was nice but we let her go to her family. They lived in
a beautiful woods. To get there we had to cross many hills and
big, big stones. We could see the Loma Mountains and Binta-
mani. You can check your map to find these mountains . . .
Everyday I go to the farms and sometimes I drive the birds so
they don't eat the rice. I use a Kuronko sling like the one Mom
gave you. I can really make it snap and hokey livin' Pete does
that stone go far."

He and his friends cooked and ate the yellow-and-black
weaver birds they killed by slingshot. Mary found pairs of pink
weaver bird feet all over the house. And gradually Aaron learned
to hunt with the men, with a shotgun, for wild boar and bush-
buck and small buffalo. They taught him to track at night. By
fourteen, despite the leopards, he was hunting alone through
the darkness. Even after a friend died of snakebite, his body going limp over Aaron's shoulder, and even after another hunter
died from a buffalo's goring, he stalked until dawn, fifteen miles
through the dense forest and elephant grass. Or he strung up
his hammock in the trees and waited beneath the moon for prey
to come. For years he'd been practicing the calls of every animal.
By now he could mimic them perfectly. He knew every hill by

heart. He "came out into the grasslands," the Kuronko phrase for hunters of high achievement. The special bamboo whistle had sounded many times before him, long, low note curling upward, announcing that he and his companions were bringing a buffalo into Foria, a buffalo he had killed. Famed as the Kuronko hunters were throughout Sierra Leone, the villagers would tell me later that he'd been as skilled as any of them. "Kuronko *Tubabu*," the people said. Kuronko White Man.

And back while Aaron was hunting with a slingshot, the older children, Matthew and Sarah, were tending their own groundnut farms, burning and clearing and tilling the ground, or trying to master the stilts of the local dancers, or trying—without much success—to translate Tolkien into Kuronko so they could read *The Hobbit* to their friends. Duko, a girl of around twelve with sad wide-set eyes, had latched on to Sarah as soon as the family arrived. In Krio, the patois that could be almost intelligible to an English speaker or that could seem as difficult as a tribal tongue, Duko asked to be her *pahdi*. Sarah could understand nothing except that perhaps Duko needed a potty. Duko tried again, signing, interlocking her two forefingers. She made herself clear at last, and soon she was teaching Sarah to count in Kuronko: "*Keleng, fila, sawa, nani . . .*" Soon she was teaching her to carry water up the steep hill from the spring, Sarah, with the village women and girls all laughing, balancing a little bowl on her head for practice. And soon the two friends were washing clothes together, slamming the wet cloth against the rocks in a system that resounded through the jungle and exhausted half the day.

"Ah, *Tubabu*," the villagers sighed, when the rice Sarah pounded spilled from the mortar. The process involved drying a meal's worth of rice in the sun, pounding it with the tapered end of the massive wooden pestle, swirling it on a woven disk to make the husks fly off, then beating again with the thick end. Her narrow face in a trance of concentration, Sarah couldn't control the pestle. When she brought it down in the center of the mortar instead of to the sides, the grains leapt out. The villagers picked them from the dirt, one by one.

But her reedy arms and shoulders grew strong, her aim exact. In an old tank top and faded wrap skirt (never liking to wear anything new, here where most everyone dressed in the Western rags that clothe much of the population of Africa), with the baby of one of her neighbor's two wives tied to her back, she helped daily in the women's unending work, all the carrying and pounding and planting, all the labor of subsistence that fell to them far more than to the men. But occasionally she and Duko, with a pack of thirty or forty women and girls, took a day's rest. They went fishing. No men were allowed. They gathered with oval nets nearly as tall as Sarah herself, and set off down the track. At the river, everyone stripped off their clothes and stomped through. For an hour they sang and churned up all the mud they could. Then, the fish blinded by murk, they walked downstream to hold out their nets, to toss the catfish and eels—dozens if they were lucky—up into the baskets they strapped on their heads, to cry out in joy.

And on her groundnut farm at harvesttime, Sarah picked up a bundle of stalks. "Snake!" Mary screamed. For a moment Sarah had no idea where it was. She was holding it in her arms, among the stalks and leaves, a puff adder, patterned in diamonds, skull broad as a fist. She dropped the bundle, lifted her machete, and sliced off the adder's head.

It had been part of Mary and Paul's hope, this immersion of their family. The immersion was far from complete. In addition to the local oven—a towering dome-shaped appliance made from the mud of termite mounds—that stood beside the house, the family had a gas stove. They had solar panels. They had a refrigerator. And the four-wheel-drive Patrol—and later a pick-up—was always parked outside, a way out. Yet the closeness that developed between the family and the villagers was essential to the kind of mission Mary and Paul had in mind, to gaining trust, to teaching rather than imposing, to introducing the small, sustainable beginnings of a new and easier life.

The bond was crucial to Paul—glasses and blond beard framing hollow cheeks—whether he was trying to introduce Christianity or trying to bring running water. He aimed for both, but perhaps for the safe water and passable roads and rudimentary health care more than the religion. The earthly things were the more immediate need. Yet he believed that one day, generations or centuries in the future, St. Paul's prophecy would come true, that "every knee will bow and every tongue confess that Jesus Christ is Lord." He saw himself helping to "claim," in tiny increments, "the world for God." There were baptisms by a stream, amidst the tangled vines and grasses that grew to fifteen feet, Paul in a T-shirt and work boots pouring a tin cup of water over a lowered head.

But there weren't nearly as many baptisms as the church back in Grand Rapids would have liked—171 in the first thirteen years, in an area with a population of around 30,000—and they weren't always of people the church would have chosen. When he felt their desire was strong enough, Paul baptized the polygamous. He saw polygamy as a difference in culture, not in devotion, a way of life (and survival, where more children meant more hands to work the farm) that he would like to change but not one that would bring damnation. And he never built a church. That would have to come from the people, when they were ready. Meanwhile he went from village to village telling Bible stories—the apple in the Garden changed to a mango; the prodigal son become a failed prospector for diamonds—under the round, open-sided shelters, the public meeting places called *tintan bohngs*.

Still, the spiritual and the earthly were not unrelated, not in Paul's mind, not in Mary's. The Kuronko, like the majority of people in Sierra Leone, were loosely Muslim but strongly ani-

mist, and while Paul and Mary had no urgent objections to
Islam, the animism seemed, to them, to instill inertia and compound hardship. It viewed the universe as swarming with capri-
cious and malign spirits; it kept the people in constant fear and
crushed almost all sense of personal will. There were spirits that
would strike you down if you walked past the wrong tree or the
wrong animal or the wrong person, failed to consult the right
seer or hire the right bush devil or make the right sacrifice.
There were spirits that would strike you down for no reason you
or your family would ever know, strike you down with maladies
Paul and Mary called tetanus or tuberculosis or amoebic dysentery. Or they might wait until you were wandering the jungle in
your animal form, then cause a hunter to shoot you, after which
you would return to your human shape for just long enough to
walk back into your village before collapsing in unmarked
death. They were responsible if your wife died in childbirth or
your baby died in infancy or your crops died in the fields, and in
the end the world was beyond human comprehension, controlled from another world that only the juju men could hope to
glimpse. Paul and Mary certainly didn't see animism as the only
factor that had kept Sierra Leone from progress. The devasta-
tions of the slave trade and the legacy of colonialism and the absence of ethical Sierra Leonean leadership and—no matter what
its causes—the reign of extreme poverty were all on their list.
But the hyperactivity of the spirits added to the air of fatalism
and paralysis, the feeling that progress could never be made.

The Kortenhovens' own religious belief was not without
the occasional intervention of invisible beings. A certain stride,
slightly long or slightly short, that kept them from stepping on a
snake they didn't notice until their foot had already come
down—such was the work of angels watching over them. And science was sometimes far off track. Evolution was undeniable but
the big bang was ludicrous; God had set everything in motion.
Yet there was a vast difference, they felt, between the onslaught
of Sierra Leonean spirits and the day-to-day distance of their

own God, who wanted mankind to take charge, to heal what had been broken in the Fall, to make the world better, to make it new.

Their small part in the remaking was a simple gravity-fed water system with eight spigots in the village of Foria. It was luring a church member from Canada, a pig farmer, to visit and help design the system. It was Paul, jack-of-all-trades minister, son of a mechanical engineer, cutting and fitting pipe and teaching the villagers as he went.

It was Mary sitting under a *tintan bohng,* training mothers what to feed their children to cure them of hepatitis, which was life threatening here, where the villagers were already in such poor health. It was Paul trying to make for drainage on the dirt road that was the area's tenuous link to the rest of Sierra Leone, the route that turned to swamp during the six months of rainy season downpour, the route toward a hospital for the man who died of TB, vomiting and coughing blood in the back of the Patrol as Mary tried to drive him toward care. ("I wish they taught a few more practical courses at seminary," Paul wrote home to his mother, "like road construction in tropical rain forests 106 instead of esoteric theology 707.") It was lobbying UNICEF to supply the measles vaccine and carrying out, after the epidemic of '83, a campaign of immunization. And it was trying to foster locally driven progress by employing and supporting men like Joseph Sesay, who worked with farmers on redesigning their fields, on rerouting the water channels so as not to waste the soil's nutrients.

Every so often a bit of remaking happened all at once.

Pa Jalloh, an old hunter in a long black-striped robe, a renowned seer with Koranic verses folded inside his amulets, had elephantiasis of the scrotum. The disease is widespread in West Africa. A mosquito transmits a dab of filarial worm larvae; the worms ruin the lymph system of the groin or leg or breast. The symptoms are usually minor swelling, a toughening of the skin. Pa Jalloh's scrotum spanned eighteen inches.

Spread-legged, he hobbled around as much as he had to. He lived eight miles from Foria, through nearly impenetrable forest. But he knew Aaron from hunting, and when he came down with a severe case of pneumonia, his friends carried him in a hammock toward the missionaries, who, getting word from a messenger, drove their pickup as close as they could. They loaded Jalloh in.

In another village, in those last years before the war, a gold-mining company had put up camp, with a gruff South African doctor whose self-styled clinic was little more than a shed. Paul knew him well, and brought Jalloh there. The doctor drowned the pneumonia in antibiotics, then offered to deal with the elephantiasis. He put Jalloh under and suspended his scrotum above the table, so he could see what he was doing. This he did by skewering the sac, in one side and out the other, and hoisting the protruding tips of steel. It wasn't only the scrotum that needed work. Its weight, about that of an uncarved pumpkin, had so dragged down the skin of the pelvis, so stretched the skin at the upper base of the penis, that the flesh had gradually descended, and the penis had been interred.

The doctor cut, lymph fluid running off the side of the table. He found the testicles deep within the mass, sponged them with saline to keep them from drying out. He pared away at hardened, fibrous tissue. He sutured the flaps of a new, normal-sized scrotum, fashioned a new sheath for the penis, and soon Pa Jalloh returned to his village, riding on the back of Aaron's motorbike.

Other help was far less dramatic. It came by introducing clotheslines so drying clothes wouldn't pick up bacteria or parasites on the ground. It came by selecting local birth attendants, equipping them with simple kits—a plastic mat, a pair of scissors, a suction syringe—and training them to clear the air passages of an unbreathing baby and to boil the string and scissors they used in cutting the umbilical cord. Mary felt she could do little,

though, about the teenage circumcision rite that left inelastic
scar tissue and could make labor a dangerous ordeal. All the
girls went through the cutting, dancing afterward from village to
village in proud celebration, hair beaded with red berries. And if
the clitoris wasn't cut deeply enough, and later their husbands
complained, they went through the cutting again. This increased
the chance of long labor and stillbirth, days of pushing until the
rectum or bladder ruptured, leaving the woman permanently in-
continent and banished from her husband's compound.

Yet Mary saw beauty in the birthing, too: a delivering woman
sitting with legs spread, leaning back against her own mother,
who in turn leaned back against the grandmother; three generations braced against one another for strength, bringing the child
into the world together, flesh to sweating flesh. In the air in
front of the daughter's swollen belly the mother danced her
hands from ribs to thighs, showing the baby the way out. Then
she stroked the daughter's breasts.

But if a baby didn't find its way, the delivering woman was
gagged with a wooden spoon to make her contractions come
harder. She might be forced to do pull-ups on the branch of a
tree or, in apparent ignorance of gravity, hung upside down by
the ankles. Often delivery took place in a latrine, so the men
couldn't see. Crying out was forbidden, so the men couldn't
hear. If the labor went on too long, if the body started to break
down, if the woman did, finally, begin to sob, she was brought
into the forest to finish her job in secret.

Mary arranged operations for women whose rectums or
bladders had torn. She urged the birthing mothers out of the latrines. It may not have been a triumph of feminist liberation, but
it cut down on infections. As did the boiled scissors, preventing
the tetanus of old razor blades. Immunization kept the measles
at bay. Still, at times the changes seemed so minimal, the problems all but infinite in size and beyond what the mission could
even attempt to address (there wasn't the financing to handle

much in the way of education, and literacy in the area hovered not far above zero percent), that the entire effort could feel a waste.

"I tend to forget about holidays sitting in the bush here," Paul wrote to his mother one Fourth of July, more than a decade into their mission. "Every day seems like the one before it and the one after it. At times the sameness of everything is almost striking. The longer we are here, the less things appear to change. Maybe that is because we are getting older. The work is still challenging and the country still beautiful, but I wonder if there will really be significant changes in this society. The mind-set of the people is both a blessing because expectations are not too great but a curse because people are so skeptical about their own ability to change for the better. Well, that's where my job comes in . . ."

The rebels weren't actually coming. It was November 1994; Sarah and Matthew had gone back to the States for college, and stayed; Paul, Mary, and Aaron remained in Foria and somehow couldn't believe the village would be attacked. Even after Joseph returned on his motorbike and described Bendugu in flames, even after the villagers packed what they could carry in bundles on their heads and hid what few other possessions they had in the jungle, even as the people began their flight, up the road or into the bush, Mary, the next morning, made the beds and folded the clothes that had been drying on the porch, as though, if she straightened the house exactly as she would have done if no war were approaching, then in fact no war would envelop them.

She intended to leave soon, but only as a precaution. She had a collection of fabric she loved, woven on the slender, elegant local looms that stretched fifteen feet from tip to shuttle, and she packed these and unpacked them, trying to decide which to take and which to leave. Her favorite was a pattern of blue, beige, and white stripes, rare because the blue was done in rich black-tinged indigo, which the weavers didn't much use anymore. She left it on the bed. Nothing was going to happen.

When the first of the wounded, a boy shot in the side, walked in from Alikalia ten miles away, the villagers still in Foria, the ones slow in packing or just coming in from their farms, entered full panic. They yelled to find children and hustled to bury rice pots in the bush and scrambled to pull on all the clothes they owned so they wouldn't be slowed by carrying anything. They ran, someone lifting the wounded boy, through an atmosphere that went from loud mayhem to vibrating silence. Aaron and Joseph carried generators and tools into the forest. Smoke rose over the closest settlements to the south. It billowed above the jungle on the nearest hill. They made trip after trip, hiding the mission's equipment so the rebels couldn't loot it. The invasion would be brief—if it came at all. Quickly they would be back to work here.

Mary left. But first she took on passengers, fifteen, twenty, slowing her down. The four-wheel-drive sagged as she headed through the swamps toward Kabala, the nearest town to the north, three hours away. Without space to cram one more adult, she stopped for babies handed through the windows. Paul and Aaron, still disbelieving even as Paul talked of somehow defending the village alongside Kuronko hunters, had refused to go, and she, enraged at their idiocy, had refused to pack them a bag; her mind, as she drove north, snagged on regret: "I should have taken a pair of underwear for Paul; he'll never think of underwear."

In Foria, a lone sprinter bolted through from another village, and cried at Aaron, "They're here! They're here! Leave, leave, leave, leave!"

Aaron raced across the village to where, in the chaos, he'd left his motorbike. He kicked down on the starter. He kicked and kicked and kicked and kicked. The engine sputtered, finally, and he churned out along with his father in the pickup and

Joseph on his Honda, each of them stopping to take on the last of the villagers. Random spurts of gunfire battered the surrounding trees, and at the crest of the next hill they turned to see the smoke above Foria, the gray spreading over green.

Aaron spent the night in Kondenbaia, partway to Kabala, with the others from Foria who'd only made it that far. In the morning he listened as artillery came closer, a deep percussion-like thunder without the fade. Paul, who'd slept in Kabala, was by then driving back toward the explosions, to gather up more of the people in flight.

Mary continued on. She'd sobbed through the night in Kabala, Paul asking her why and she wondering who she was married to. "What am I crying for? You know that is probably the dumbest question I've ever heard." She reminded him that most of the families they'd lived with for fourteen years were now, in the darkness, hiding with their children in the bush in a downpour. And that the Sierra Leone Army was unable and probably unwilling to defend anyone or anything—probably even Kabala where the soldiers were stationed. And that their own son was back there somewhere, maybe not in the bush but nowhere safe.

She headed out. She'd had enough. She shared a farewell Coke with Aaron when he surfaced the next day in Kabala, then told her husband and son, "See you in Freetown." Her anger was gone. She just knew she needed to leave, needed to find safety, needed to call Sarah and Matthew, to talk with the half of her family that was far away and in no danger. And she knew Paul and Aaron did not share her needs, that she could not convince them, could not even ask them at this moment when all their lives had entered an impossible extreme—a place where need grew pure—to go with her, to give up what they needed to do.

"See you in Freetown." That was all. It was something she still struggled to explain, years later. "You think there should be big tears and goodbyes . . . All I knew was that I wasn't going to stick around in Kabala . . . We didn't know what was coming . . ."

She locked the doors of the four-wheel-drive and started—

alone, telling none of the villagers and taking no one with her—toward the capital. At a roadblock at the edge of Kabala, the gatekeeper raised the wooden pole. A pack of government soldiers ordered it down. They tried to commandeer the vehicle. AK-47s and hand-held grenade launchers at her windows, they told her it was her duty to her people. Quietly, she said no. They told her repeatedly. "I've already done a lot for my people," she said in her small voice, and apparently the gatekeeper, who had seen her come through with fleeing villagers the day before, agreed. The consequence for him she never knew. He lifted the pole and she floored the gas.

Paul and Aaron, for the next day and a half, helped set up a camp in Kabala to feed the families running from their homes and flooding the town; they spread a map and showed a government army major exactly how the R.U.F. would approach Kabala; they drove the pickup back again toward the rebel advance, rescuing whoever couldn't make it out on foot. Then, figuring the R.U.F. was still a few miles away, Paul, Aaron, and Joseph sat on the newly abandoned grounds of another church's mission school. In the town below, the Tamaboros, a Kuronko militia, put out word that they had encircled Kabala with white thread and that the rebels could not enter. On the hilltop, Paul, Aaron, and Joseph found some Cokes in the school refrigerator and debated what to do next. The first shots came in a three-beat cluster. They came from the hill's base, from the side of the rebels' approach.

Aaron had one of his hunting rifles with him. For a moment, he thought about taking it along in flight. Paul and Joseph said no; if he was captured it would only make things worse. Then the government soldiers erupted with AKs and artillery. Smoke clouded the trees. They unleashed a heavy machine gun. Thousands of rounds tore into the hill. The R.U.F. pounded the opposite bank, maneuvering around it. It would seem later, after the rebels had overrun the town, to have been almost a fake battle, filled with wild fire and acquiescence—or partial collusion—

by government troops. From where they were, they never had much chance of hitting the enemy. But Aaron and Paul and Joseph, with an old Sierra Leonean school guard who'd appeared along with them, were trapped at the crest.

Maybe the safest thing would have been to lie at the top, escape later. But no one wanted to be caught by the rebels. Aaron plunged down the hill, picking a face as safe as possible in the crossfire. The drop was steep, almost a cliff, and he reeled down through the vines, scuttling to the base. Then he crouched, ready to flee, Joseph and the old man with him. His father yelled from the top. From seventy yards straight up, Paul hollered through the barrage, through the wall of noise.

His hand broken not long before, Paul had just come back from surgery in the States. Fifty years old, he couldn't see surviving it down that pitch with only one hand to grab at underbrush. He couldn't force himself over the precipice. At the bottom, just above the three men, bullets ripped through the leaves. Aaron started climbing. He reached his father, let Paul brace his weight against him. They slid and scraped their way to the base.

A rocket-propelled grenade struck near the school where they'd been seconds earlier. Aaron's knees buckled, from the impact on air and ground, from fear. He chased Joseph ahead, ordered him, when Joseph protested, not to slow down, told him that if Aaron and the two older men didn't make it, Joseph would be able to send out a search. And Joseph, deciding wisely that no matter what the rebels had done with a few whites in the southeast, his own prospects if he waited and was caught were far worse than his employers', took off. The RPGs kept coming. Aaron and Paul and the old man ducked forward. Rounds drilled into tree trunks. Dirt spattered near their shins. The firing came mostly from the government side, seemed almost random, spread wide and scarcely aimed, but the three men couldn't tell if the troops had spotted them, mistaken the whites for rebel mercenaries. They crossed a path, exposed; kept scrambling, low. More bombardment. They crawled, squirmed, lay tight to the ground when they heard the hissing before the explosions, the shrapnel. Paul started to cough. He couldn't breathe. The assault was constant. He needed to stand, at least lift his chest off the ground, get some air into his lungs. Aaron pinned his father down.

The artillery quieting, the machine-gunning rampant, they edged forward again. A spot of red caught Aaron's eyes. The men froze. Fifty yards into the elephant grass, it flickered and vanished, the red on the sleeve of a military policeman. Paralyzed, the men waited for him to open fire. Minutes went by before a red bishop bird shot out at them.

They raced ahead, reaching a soccer field, clinging to a concrete wall before trying to cross. The R.U.F. had shifted around the hill, ready to overtake the town, no longer shooting in the direction of the fleeing men. The wall was safety, except for what the rebels would do to their bodies if they waited too long and were trapped in Kabala and captured. All the firing came from the opposite side. From houses a few hundred yards away, government troops blasted across the soccer field, blasted at empty forest. Aaron said he would go first. The instant he leapt out from behind the wall he would be a target. Head low, he ran for the sea of towering grass waiting on the far sideline. It folded him in. Then he watched his father start across the open expanse.

It had been two hours, two hours of slithering and hunching and darting since they'd left the hilltop, but now, at last, in the sea of grass and beyond, the three men were outside the line of fire. The battle was barely behind them, but by the standards they'd come to know, danger was hundreds of miles away. The guns roared. Beside a swamp Paul told his son, "Thanks for saving my life," and then they came to the camp for the displaced, abandoned clothing and cooking pots littering the ground. A lone lunatic woman railed in Krio that everyone should have stayed, "I tell dem make dem no run, me I done sit down here, notting go wrong wid we." By dark the men had joined the exo-

dus on the road outside town. Paul and Aaron were interrogated
by a pair of government soldiers pointing an AK-47 and a
grenade launcher, and later, hearing gunfire on the road and a
car racing close, they thought it was filled with rebels and dove
into the bush. Walking again, Paul's hand throbbed. So they
went miles in single file, son in front of father, Paul's forearm
propped high on Aaron's shoulder. Steps awkwardly synchro-
nized, bodies joined, they passed a cripple who'd set out from
Foria three days earlier. His knees were twisted by polio. His
matchstick legs were in permanent crook. Feet flopping at right
angles to his relentless stride, he pointed as well as he could
point and told them: "Go."

Paul and Mary and Aaron were living again in Foria by Christmas, trucking in food and medicine. The villagers were rebuild-
ing. The rebels had only torn through: occupation would come
later, after other attacks.

The Kortenhovens fled and returned, fled and returned,
and finally, when the route from Freetown to Foria became, even
in their judgment, too dangerous to travel, they stayed in the
capital, setting up a shelter for women victimized by the war,
women with the babies of rape, women with the R.U.F.'s initials
carved into their breasts.

As the government army ransacked the capital in 1997,
Aaron was at college in Ohio. Paul and Mary remained in Freetown, bunkered in their house by the bay. The walls soaked up
bullets. Mary pulled a chair into the dressing room, putting two
walls between herself and the war. A band of soldiers strolled
down the driveway. Paul went out to meet them, to pay them off
so they wouldn't take the car. They took his money the first time,
took the car the second. Drunk, the third pack of soldiers told
Paul they would make him part of their "Supreme Council."

Even with Paul's heart, as he put it, "slowly biting the dust,"
forcing him to undergo surgery back in the States, he and Mary

kept on in Sierra Leone. Aaron returned for a year after college. Led by Mary, they conceived a women's center in Kabala, to teach literacy and basic math and cloth-dyeing, to turn victims into businesswomen, wretched lives in a crushed town into the start of a new economy, even a hint of equality. But beyond whether their project could make any difference, what I needed to understand, as we shared dinner in the bullet-riddled house or drove into rebel-held Foria, was how this couple and their youngest son could feel such a deep connection to this nation that no level of risk could chase them away. Yes, the risk was itself a draw, a thrill, and yes, Paul took an open pride in his survival, but their voices didn't quicken all that much as they recounted their escapes. Why didn't they just leave? Hadn't they done enough to satisfy their longing to do good? Why didn't they go home, or at least go to do good somewhere easier, somewhere safer? I needed to know, because at times I felt no connection at all to the country—nothing but the inexorable clutch of a nightmare—and I recoiled from their caring. It seemed, then, that there was no solution to the existence of a place like Sierra Leone except to return home and ignore its existence altogether.

SEVEN "Mr. Al Gore said the people of America should pray for Mr. George Bush and pray for his family. And then Mr. George Bush said pray for Mr. Al Gore. I was very much moved. In fact, I was very much happy. There was a little argument, they go to court everyday, but everything was smooth. Cool and calm."

Lamin had traveled to New York in November 2000. He stayed until February. A New Jersey real estate investor and a Brooklyn prosthetist had seen, separately, photographs of Sierra Leone's amputees in *The New York Times*, and had wound up, together, flying five men across the Atlantic to be fitted with hands. Lamin, living in a fetid camp for the maimed and their families, where human will often seemed to have been cut off with the limbs of the residents, had lobbied hard with the head of the camp to be chosen as one of the five.

"Even when they were going to court," he remembered watching the aftermath of the election on the small TV in the room he and another amputee shared at a YMCA, "you could have heard that they cause a big catastrophe—they have killed somebody, they have cut hands, cut legs, a lot of nonsense. My brothers in Sierra Leone said the only way they would be able to achieve power was to go into the bush, to come and burn people's houses, killing people, cutting people. To rule people. In fact, watching Mr. George Bush and Mr. Al Gore, I have cried. Of course I did. Because that is the reason we are here. Because that is the reason we are amputated today.

"If it would have been our country," he went on, "even when Mr. George Bush was declared winner he could have given orders to go and fight the people of Mr. Al Gore. But America is a superpower. They can rule the people perfectly."

There were other things to marvel at. The YMCA, in Greenpoint, Brooklyn, had a preschool off the bright, clean lobby; the kids' cubbies, outside the classroom's plate glass doors, were labeled with neat strips of white tape. Behind the spotless glass, children played in a carefully architected universe formed of wooden tiers and little ladders and colorful chairs. "Ashes, ashes," they sang high in their cleverly sectioned space, "we all fall down!"

Behind more glass stood the gleaming geometry of exercise machines, and the outer vestibule held stacks of blue and pink flyers for classes called "Health and Wellness Orientation" and "Forever Young."

Past the reception desk was the door leading upstairs to the rooms the men occupied. The door's handle had been changed as soon as they arrived. The first day, it had been a steel sphere, which the men, with their stumps or the crude, almost useless prosthetics Lamin had managed to get for himself from one of the aid agencies in Freetown, could not possibly turn. Immediately a lever replaced it. And beyond the vestibule filled with flyers, outside and across the street, were the dozen shiny blue-and-white cars of the neighborhood police station, all parked at a uniform angle.

To navigate between the Y and the diner where the amputees' meals had been prepaid took concentration. Lamin oriented himself by a Radio Shack, checked his memory by the other bedazzling storefronts (George's Variety Shop with its window display of coffeemakers; the Polish groceries and Polish video shops of one of New York's modest and unbedazzling neighborhoods) to his left and right, before attempting the block and a half. The diner's menu overwhelmed as well. For eleven weeks, he and the others ordered one of two luxuries, chicken with rice or beef with rice. They tasted strawberry jello early on and stuck with that every night for dessert.

Their usual waitress, a woman around sixty, with a close helmet of blond hair, was staggered at first, too. "Are these people

human beings?" she asked about the men who had done the cutting, when the maimed told their story. "Yes," Lamin said, "they
are human beings." She helped to feed them before they got
their new limbs, and afterward as they learned to use them.
For one man, too despondent to master the prosthetics, she
spooned rice into his mouth for months. "I was afraid," she recalled, voice raspy and face carved and lined. "I didn't know if I
could do it. I'd never fed anyone before except a baby." She was
Polish, and I asked if what had happened to the men made her
think of the horrors Poland had been through, the Stalin era
suffering I'd seen memorialized in neighborhood window displays. "It happens everywhere," she sighed. "It's life. It's life."

Among the marvels, for Lamin, were the city's construction
sites. With a social worker he met amidst the thin network of
help and friendship that grew up around the men, he sought
out countless foundation pits and half-finished high-rises. It was
Lamin's request. He liked to gaze at the bulldozers and cranes,
and at the towers climbing behind their intricate scaffoldings
of steel, dwarfing Freetown's five- or six-story hulks, seared and
bullet-pocked, that had been built with scaffoldings of bamboo
poles. New York's fabulous structures were signs: of the white
man's control over evil spirits, so that the forces of the underworld were made to build up the white's country rather than de-
stroying it. It was similar, he thought, to the training of a puppy
he watched one afternoon during his trip, a pet scarcely resembling the wild dogs and half-tamed guard animals of his home. "I
saw a dog playing ball! Really!" he remembered. "I was very
much surprised. Even when I told my colleagues, the others of
the amputees, they said get out."

Between sessions with the prosthetist, the men were taken to
see *The Lion King*, a spectacle that didn't make much of an impression, and to the top of the Empire State Building, which
made, on Lamin, the greatest impression of all. He stared out at
the suspension bridges and the Twin Towers. He felt the unimag-
inable December wind, felt the building tremble and still stand,

and then the men were led to the Waldorf-Astoria, shown the lobby of grand chandeliers and the massive clock with the golden replica of the Statue of Liberty in the hotel where American presidents stayed.

But on their way from the Empire State Building to the Waldorf, their tour guide for that day, a staffer from Human Rights Watch, thought they would like to see the famous Christmas windows at Lord & Taylor. She hadn't yet seen the exhibit herself— it featured a kind of anarchic circus theme, with chimey music and blinking lights and with spilling popcorn. In one window, colored bowling pins were juggled by a manic six-armed boy. In another, a pair of immense white-gloved hands, cut off at the wrists, one of them severed in a zigzag pattern, juggled a helpless bowtied man and his ragdoll date. The hands were eight times the size of everything else in the display, except for a giant laughing mouth, bodiless as the grotesque hands themselves. Staring, Lamin's mind went back to the little cane figures he had made in primary school, the *falu* doll that earned him a mark of 85 percent. He thought that were it not for what had happened, he might have been able to make better clowns than those in the window. "Then people would say, Oh, who made this?" he imagined. "I would have that praise . . ."

They didn't stay long at the windows, so dominated by arms, hands. "We proceeded ahead, because the more we would continue to look, the more we would get discouraged in our hearts."

Above all else, they had wanted to know one thing as they sat for the first time in the prosthetist's office: Would they be able to use the bathroom by themselves?

"If you could for a moment—and it's almost impossible to do—imagine yourself without hands," the prosthetist told me later, "it's so overwhelmingly disabling. If you've lost one hand you can be almost completely functional and independent. But to have lost both hands . . ." The amputees were traveling with two male Sierra Leonean chaperones, who had to tend to everything. "It puts you at such an absolute disadvantage in terms of the most basic necessities, and going to the bathroom is one of them. And these are not children. These are men. The psychological impact is tremendous."

The prosthetist told them they would.

But here in this land of superpower, where witchcraft facilitated science, the men expected everything restored. They had heard of the electric nerves, the surface that looked exactly like skin, the five fingers that could do everything you had once done with your own.

Sitting with the men around the burnished wood of his conference table, the prosthetist told them they would not be receiving that type of device. The parts would break down and be impossible to fix in Sierra Leone. The batteries would run out. He explained that although they looked like real hands, only three of the five fingers actually worked. And because an artificial limb was controlled by information coming only from the eyes, not at all through touch, the bulky cosmetic hands, whose skin was useless except for appearance, made translating the commands of the brain much more difficult. Even here in the United States, people chose the most streamlined hand if they wanted the best function. He showed the men the metal claw: A pair of curved steel pincers extended from a forearm of brown plastic. When operated by a steel cable that ran along the forearm, the pincers snapped open and shut.

Lamin felt the blood draining out of him, felt he was dying all over again.

And one of the men, once a teacher, never recovered from that moment. When the soldiers had seized him, he'd begged them to leave at least his left hand, the one he wrote with. Now, back at the Y after the initial meeting with the prosthetist, he wilted in the director's office and told her he could never learn to hold chalk again, not with the hands he would be given. And a year later I saw him nearly catatonic in the amputee camp, his stumps bare, his prosthetics unused for months and missing their screws.

At a Brooklyn hospital Lamin went through rehabilitation classes every day. He learned to work himself into the harness that fit across his shoulders. At the center of the canvas straps, between his shoulder blades, lay a small metal ring. From there the single cables, what Lamin called "the veins," ran down each plastic forearm. Slowly, through endless practice, Lamin learned to shift his shoulders in the particular subtle ways that caused the two fingers of his right hand to open wide or narrow, close soft or tight. Slowly he learned the same with his left. Slowly he learned to use the mechanism that could bend his wrists back, letting him grasp at varied angles. Slowly he learned to eat without food spilling off his spoon, to drink a cup of tea, to fill an entire page with legible sentences. But before he came even close to mastering those skills, he rode the subway with his parka sleeves rolled up, one plastic limb raised high, pincers clasping the handle.

"I wanted people to see that I have complete hands," he said, "that I'm able to do something for myself."

He had something more than determination. He had a kind of resourcefulness the other men didn't seem to possess, a quality that came close to aggression, not in any physical way but in its quiet, unflagging persistence as he asked for money. He asked the staff at the Y and the members of a nearby church and the social worker who took him to construction sites and a novelist he met through Human Rights Watch. The others asked and were given modest amounts; Lamin asked over and over and was given far more. He seemed to have no hesitancy about his requests, to treat his fundraising almost as matter of factly as a job, speaking of his family, his six children, to the same person for the seventh time, "not at all shy," as the Y's director put it, "about letting you know what he needed." When he suggested repeatedly that the Y should finance new housing for him back home, she held him off, trying to explain what she feared, to him, must be inconceivable, that no matter how terrible things were in Sierra Leone, the organization had priorities here, poverty here, "children of prostitutes and drug addicts, right here on the south side, even if it looks like we have everything."

But with the novelist, a single gray-haired woman living in two quaint rooms on the Upper East Side, his fundraising was more successful. She gave him $5,000. And though in the time after his amputation nothing more than a vague ambition had resolved him to stay alive—a sense that he might still accomplish something though he didn't know what his ruined body would allow—now his goals had come clear. He began to build.

Gunshots came from downtown. "Turn around, turn around, there is firing," people screamed at the cars on the inbound routes, screamed needlessly, because the traffic was already in a state of madness, trying wildly to reverse itself though there was no space to move, as rattling pickup trucks full of U.N. soldiers, guns raised, barreled down the hill. People ran, climbing, fleeing Freetown's center. ("Follow the soldiers," I told Foday, my driver. "This is my life," he said. "I know you journalists." Anytime I started thinking life was cheap here, I had to reckon with what I knew of Foday, who seemed to value existence highly enough. "You go there by foot.") Market women, wares abandoned, raced past the roundabout, away from the ancient cotton tree with the vultures in its branches and the "Love One Another Campaign" placard below. Schoolgirls in their blue dresses, some with faces washed by terror, others laughing like American kids in a chaotic fire drill, sprinted past the billboard that announced, "National Longterm Perspective Studies: Sierra Leone Vision 2025 Official Launching Ceremony." The packed vans with their painted slogans—"The More You Hate the More God Bless," "Together as One," "No Condition is Permanent"—sped by the graffiti that read "Body Count" and the U.S. Embassy where ninety-odd windows had been shot out during the last coup.

Over by the national prison, where the soldiers had opened the gates during previous uprisings, and where a billboard rose beside the high wall—"Guinness. The Power. See it. Feel it. Taste it."—the panic had started with government paramilitaries firing warning shots outside the walls during trouble within. Then the U.N. troops added their influence, shooting into the air as well. It hadn't been much, but in a city always waiting to be overrun, it hadn't taken much to set off a stampede that left two people trampled to death.

That was the way the city was: It slept—the heat-drugged machine gunners dozing behind the dusty sandbag igloos of their checkpoints—and then it woke in a frenzy.

I'd been scheduled to meet Lamin that morning downtown. When I found him later, face slackened by apathy, he said he hadn't rushed anywhere at the sound of the shots. He'd stood listless on a corner, letting the thousands crush past, until he was virtually alone. "I am halfway done," he thought. "If they come to finish me I don't mind."

The apathy didn't last. He found land in his old neighborhood of Kissy. For the shallow foundation he hired boys as diggers and sometimes worked his own shovel, however weak the thrusts. His crew staked slender iron rods into the ground, wavering formations that looked to me no sturdier than trellises. He bought unweighed sand sold vaguely by the pickup load and stones sold by the headpan (stones collected, one by one throughout the country, by stooped women who then piled their rocks in tiny pyramids by the roadside and prayed for a merchant to drive along and buy them); he purchased rotting planks and rusty nails and old cardboard. The boys tore the cardboard into strips and nailed it between the planks. This was the structure of the ceiling. Over damp, disintegrating cardboard the cement floor of the second story would be spread.

He planned two sprawling stories, twelve bedrooms, four verandas, apartments to rent. There would be an indoor kitchen for his wife, indoor toilets, showers somehow hooked to Kissy's nearest water line, which offered a public spigot a hundred yards away. "People will say, This man hasn't got any hands and he is putting up such a building!" His family would never again live in the camp, the voluntary, fenced jail of will-less prisoners, of glazed eyes and rank mud and limp bodies and bare stumps whose healed flesh looked water-logged.

There, in the camp, in his hut of plastic sheeting, he had a recurring dream—an unknown woman talking to him, his natural hands returned to him, and he touching her while she talked—a dream worse than a nightmare when he woke. But M-A, his wife, had been kind. They had a new baby, Bartholomeus. "You know," Lamin confided over beers one afternoon, his fingers seeming to grip the neck of a bottle as effortlessly as my own did, "even a blind man can have a wife, and she, too, can produce children. I don't see why an amputee cannot do the same thing. My hands were chopped off and not my—" We laughed.

He and M-A slept with the prosthetics dangling from a pole directly above their bed. The minute he woke, he put the harness over his shoulders and his left stump into its plastic limb. With the left pincers he pulled a dingy sock up to his right bicep, straightened the sock, and slipped the right arm into its prosthetic, which he then used to smooth a sock onto his left. "I have become part of these limbs. I can't move without them. I feel very much ashamed when people see me with my ordinary stumps outside." Easily both sets of pincers took the bottom hem of a T-shirt and tugged it over his head. The T-shirt said "Speedway" and showed a checkered flag. He pulled on gray slacks, fastened and zipped them.

"As soon as I have the determination in my heart," he described how automatic the skills had become, "then my heart will send it to the brain . . . " He folded a scrap of fabric for a hand-kerchief, tucked it into his pocket, and stepped outside.

Caught in a slant of early sunlight, a woman with a face of arresting beauty, all lovely angles and copper-tinted skin, slouched armless against a wooden post. A one-armed mother tried to bathe her baby. Lamin sat near his wall of white sheeting, holding Bartholomeus against his chest. Soon, with plaited hair and a plastic Mickey Mouse backpack, Rugiatu clutched his hand on the way to school. And later, at his construction site, he snipped an iron rod to size with a pair of large corroded clippers.

One evening we walked downtown again, shopping. I, too, heard his requests for help and, adhering cruelly to a reporter's rules, refused them, except for some occasional food. We walked into a small shop, and there, for the price of the 5,000 leone note—about two dollars—that I'd just given him, I saw an act of magic more powerful than any white witchcraft he imagined that my country possessed.

He bought a container of mango juice. The owner set down his change. Then, having taught himself so exquisitely well, Lamin plucked a coin, scarcely thicker than a penny, off the glass counter.

EIGHT "The African knows no peace," Lord Frederick Lugard, British imperial officer, subjugator and ruler from Uganda to Nigeria, wrote at the turn of the twentieth century. "One day you may see peace and plenty, well-tilled fields, and children playing in the sun; on the next you may find the corpses of the men, the bodies of the children half burnt in the flames which consumed the village, while the women are captives of the victorious raiders . . . The *Pax Britannica* which shall stop this lawless raiding and constant inter-tribal war will be the greatest blessing that Africa has known since the Flood."

It was hard, a century later, not to sense reverberations of the past within the British training, where the firepower demonstrations recalled Lugard's rallying of his African recruits with fearsome displays of his Maxim machine guns. It was hard not to hear it in the British tents in the jungle, where a sergeant, cleaning his gun, explained the evil that had gradually overtaken Sierra Leone since independence—"somewhere along the line the dark side took over," and hard not to hear it at government defense headquarters, where a British colonel predicted, "A hundred of us could finish the R.U.F. fast": he hoped his own government would set him free from training an army and patrolling territory not far from the capital, that he and a small, gunship-backed force of British soldiers would be allowed to fight the war offensively, to take on a ragtag enemy numbering 10,000 to 15,000, to destroy evil themselves.

But a part of the past seemed gone. For Lugard had believed that favorable trade with Africa would make England's "blessing" a source of profit. The forces of "commerce and Christianity," the explorer David Livingstone had declaimed, would work together to upraise the heathens. In Sierra Leone, this program had been carried forward by British governors (one came straight from fighting the Zulus in South Africa) and British commanders, who led Sierra Leonean paramilitaries in marches of suppression. When villages refused to pay a hut tax, when warriors slaughtered white missionaries and traders in protest, a thousand were mowed down in battle, a hundred hung. The tax was meant to spur the output of palm oil, to prod the villagers from "the laziness which prevails everywhere," as one District Commissioner saw it, "to rouse them from their apathy and indolence and to bring them more in touch with civilizing influences." The marches were used, as well, in trying to intimidate the people into abandoning their clan warfare, their traditional slavery, the practices of their Leopard Societies. "They said they would give their own children in return for mine," a witness recounted at a British-run trial of Society members in 1904. "They begged me too much. They said they would fine me four heads of money . . . They said in two days' time they would catch the child . . . It was dark night. They called me by a whistle and I went. Banna Sokie . . . was dressed in a leopard skin . . . Banna Sokie gripped the child with the knife . . . We took the child down to a swamp by the river . . . cut off the legs at the thighs and the arms . . . Each took a part of the meat . . . I took a part and ate it." The British felt they would save the people from themselves.

The great profits of conquest never materialized in territories like Sierra Leone—the colony scarcely exported enough raw materials to stay solvent; and without much of a cash economy, Sierra Leoneans couldn't provide the new market England had visions of finding for its industrial goods. Still, financial promise had been part of the imperial incentive. A hundred years later, in the current mission, there didn't appear to be any such motive. Sierra Leone had enough diamonds to fund a low-tech third-world civil war, but—as opposed to a commodity like crude oil—the first world had no pressing need for more diamonds. (The gem had long been stockpiled by the mining giant

De Beers to keep supply artificially low and prices artificially high.) Someday, 200 to 300 million dollars' worth of diamonds might possibly be exported each year from the country (an estimate that depended not only on peace but on expensive mechanization and mine security and, too, elusive controls on smuggling). It wasn't enough to raise credible suspicions of neo-colonial exploitation.

There was heroism in the British effort, risk without the promise of tangible reward. And there was palpable enthusiasm. In the British tents, I heard hardly a note of bitterness about this deluged and far-flung assignment. "What I'd like by Christmas," said the sergeant who'd spoken of the "dark side," "is to beat the bloody R.U.F. out of the diamond fields, put this country right on its feet." And here and there, I heard even a voice of humility. "We've got to be careful not to develop a God syndrome," Sergeant Furlong said, forgoing his Gortex so he would get drenched with his trainees. "We're not the white man on a pedestal."

Yet always there was the old wish to be an agent of salvation (stoked, to some unknowable degree, by Britain's modern worries of diminished status in the world), and always there was an unmitigated confidence, a sense of invincibility that, though I hadn't heard the men speak in explicitly racist terms, was surely at least tinged by race. Captain Rosenfeld, brand-new to Africa but feeling well briefed on indigenous warfare, described the local style of fighting: "First there's firing and then everyone runs. Whoever runs the least far wins." And his commander, Major Alan Marshall, put the training goal like this: "We don't have to turn them into good Western soldiers. Just good African soldiers."

"Breeteeesh!" the kids cheered, when the patrols came through their villages thirty-five miles outside Freetown. They did a skipping, side-stepping dance between the pair of Land Rovers, the eight or ten soldiers, the machine gun on its pivot—between that and their burnt homes. "Breeteeesh! Breeteeesh! Bree-teeesh!"

But it wasn't only the kids, and the Sierra Leonean adults, who were cheering. Kofi Annan, the United Nation's Ghanaian secretary general, knew the futility of his own troops in establishing control. The U.N.'s peacekeeping missions basically rented their soldiers from member nations, and no first-world country had been willing to lease out its battalions for the sake of Sierra Leone. "You know that countries which supplied us with soldiers were supposed to equip them fully and train them well," Annan said. "Some soldiers arrived without even a uniform." Whether poor nations dispatched their men for the sake of revenue or valorous reputation, they had sometimes sent them to Sierra Leone without helmets, without rifles. Annan wished the U.K. would put its troops under U.N. command. But about the way England had surged in, creating a province of tenuous order around the capital, his spokesperson for Africa, Marie Okabe, told me, "It's their presence that is making the difference."

The Land Rovers stopped beside a surreal plant, its eight-foot leaves so perfectly fan-shaped it seemed on the verge of spinning. The rain had paused. Things felt almost relaxed, as though trouble were in the next country and not the next town. The people took the British to be at least as invincible as the British took themselves. "Look at me," the village chief said quietly to the head of the patrol. His remaining teeth had caved inward. Twig-thin beneath shredded slacks and a candy-striped shirt that might, in another life seven lives ago, have been sold behind a counter at Brooks Brothers, he stood beside a mission school, torched and sinking into the bush. "And this for a headman." He touched his clothes while his other hand clutched a plastic baggie used so long it was barely clear. Inside was a grade-school report card of his daughter's, disintegrating, like an artifact of an ancient dream. "I am too happy you British are here. I am tired. We can rest."

Not only rest but any chance of recovery was, people felt, up
to the onetime masters. "It's a sad situation, very sad," Abdul
Tejan-Cole, a Freetown lawyer, internationally honored as an activist for human rights and improved governance, said, as we
talked of peace and of structuring a functional society. "All of
our faith is in foreigners, in the British. My grandfather, who
fought for independence, would be turning over in his grave."
But dedicated as Tejan-Cole himself was to rescuing his country,
he didn't feel the faith was misplaced. At least, he didn't see
much alternative as he spoke about the nation's pervasive corruption and collapsed governmental institutions, its legal system
"that was the envy of West Africa in the '60s" and that was all but
nonexistent now, and about a loss of conscience that affected the
entire society. "Morally," he said, "the culture has gone to zero."

Hinga Norman, deputy minister for defense and head of the
Civil Defense Forces, put it not so differently. "There is no wis-
dom without realistic understanding of the facts," he said, then
spoke as if the British were beside us: "You were in control of our
nation. You left a nice arrangement, and eventually by ourselves
we spoiled it. Please come again and help us."

Lamin, like so many, went one long step further: "Take a
child in school. If he cannot understand what you are teaching
him, he needs to get back so that you can teach him more. So I,
for one, want the British to come rule us once more again."

As ever, I asked about anger for the past, stressed that most
Americans would expect Africans to feel that.

"Well, angry with somebody who has come, who wants to put
something in your brain, somebody who is your teacher? How
can you be angry with your teacher? If you become angry with
your teacher and your teacher becomes annoyed with you, then
he will leave you and you will not know anything. And so when
you go and knock your head on the rock, then you will crawl to
get back to him. Teacher, please come to my aid. I think that is
what led us today—we are unable to take care of ourselves. It's

better that we get back to our master so they could handle the situation."

And a building contractor out in Bo, a white-haired man dressed in fine African fabrics and old enough to have spent his childhood under English rule, told his friends in his unlit, un-busy office, "I am for recolonization. I don't care if you drive a Rolls-Royce, so long as I can drive a Toyota as well." He would tolerate racial injustice for the sake of reasonable living.

Only one of the five men in the room, a secondary school teacher, disagreed. Voice rising, he reminded that before inde-pendence, "We had segregation, right over there, we couldn't go to that school!"

"At least there *was* school for Africans," the contractor said. "They care for all their subjects."

The teacher laughed in high-pitched, angry amazement. "They deceive you! And the white man that colonized you, he is only the great, great grandparent of *this* white man!"

"No, these white men care about us," the contractor insisted.

And somewhere beneath it all, lurking close or far below such sentiments, was what lay atop the heads of the street sellers walking with their assorted wares piled high on round trays. Amidst the soap and biscuits were tubes of Tenovate. The cream, containing a potent steroid, was sold by prescription in the West to treat only severe skin diseases. Here old tubes of the medi-cine, at a dollar or two each, were used to assault the skin and turn it a few shades closer to white.

The Tenovate; the other makeshift blanching creams on sale at the market stalls; the homemade chemical bleaches people talked about—they shouldn't have surprised me. But they did, here in Africa. More than in New York, the skin-lightening seemed to expose a sense of inferiority that ran unspeakably deep.

Then there was its opposite: the sense of superiority, no less deep and no more rational, across the racial divide. Without it, I sometimes thought, the British wouldn't have felt such absolute confidence in such foreign terrain, even with all their actual superiority in technology and training. It was inside me, too. Out on patrol with the British, I felt that nothing could touch me.

Of the village chief displaying his daughter's old report card, the patrol asked if there'd been any trouble in the area, any sign of the West Side Boys. The British had armed the West Side Boys several weeks earlier (shortly after Komba had left the militia). It had seemed, then, that the group had turned against the rebels. But its new allegiance hadn't lasted. The militia had splintered, and a faction of about 300 was presently dreaming of Kabbah's overthrow while strafing busses and gang-raping women twenty miles northeast of where the patrol now was. To secure the area—including the British tents at the training base nearby— the British needed to know if the militia had been coming through.

The chief said there had been a spate of robberies, that he thought it was the West Side Boys. The British—rifles strapped to their backs rather than in their hands, an intentional sign of friendliness, of outreach in a foreign land, but also a hint of unconcern—didn't ask the chief for any details. And the chief, deferent, didn't offer what wasn't requested. The patrollers strolled back to their vehicles, as though the few of them could eliminate the entire faction if it ever came around to try anything more serious.

The Land Rovers crept on along the rutted tracks. They passed coconut trees and the brilliant green tendrils of swamp rice, so thick and even the swamps seemed covered in plush carpet. They passed graffiti on a mud wall: "War Is My Food." They returned to the base, a spot which had been overrun twice during the last three years and where now, with the rain starting again and turning the parade ground into a pond, the trainees cried:

"Sah!"

"Listeennn to me!"

Behind Captain Rosenfeld sat a government army paymaster, in charge of handing the men bricks of badly devalued cash. He drew the bricks from a burlap rice sack. The pay amounted to about thirty dollars per month, but when it came to money, the dismally low salary was only half the problem in keeping these soldiers loyal. The other half was that senior officers, from men like the paymaster to those all the way up the line, took extra helpings from the burlap bags to supplement their own meager pay. Historically, the men at the bottom often got nothing much at all. Indeed the paymaster was today turning away some trainees, telling them brusquely that he couldn't find their names on his hand-scrawled lists. They accepted his rulings without protest. But the British captain had just upbraided him, ordered him to look harder through his bedraggled sheets.

"You *will* be paid!" Rosenfeld boomed out to the men, standing on the paymaster's platform above them.

"Sah!"

"Do you hear me?"

"Sah!"

"I said, You will be paid!"

"Sah!"

"Are you happy?"

"Sah!"

And this was crucial to the British certainty that they could remake the country, working outward from the military. (Kabbah had asked them to take over the army officially; the British had accepted the role without the appointment, their top brass sitting tight beside a Sierra Leonean chief of staff.) In fostering an uncorrupt army they would foster a disciplined and loyal one, constructed of officers who would "lead to serve their men," Rosenfeld said, and of soldiers "who feel themselves different from the rebels, who feel a desire to serve society." It sounded so plausible in his upbeat voice, almost as straightforward as an equation.

And as for the hardened war criminals whom steady pay

couldn't soften, there were two more remedies. One was a great deal of precision marching, replete with a certain twisted angle of the neck when standing rigid in formation. The parade drill might seem a waste of time, the instructors explained, but it was a way to build spirit in a soldier's heart. The other remedy was the British military chaplain. After negotiating a mock battle-field of explosives and barbed wire, of riddling British gunners aiming over their heads, the trainees sat under a tree, grenades going off in the background, for a session of preaching. Or rather, the chaplain didn't preach but read from a booklet, pudgy face and blue eyes lowered toward the text, never lifting toward the men, who sat dazed before him. "If in the course of battle," he droned in language incomprehensible to most of them, "you encounter any individual of whose status you are uncertain . . ."

Within a few weeks, the West Side Boys took eleven British pa-trollers hostage.

There had been a perceived slackening in West Side Boys' activity, and Major Marshall—"We don't have to turn them into good Western soldiers. Just good African soldiers"—led a patrol past the area where he was authorized to go, likely figuring that no one in the British hierarchy would ever object; that he and his crew would survey an extra stretch of jungle from their three-vehicle caravan, their Browning machine gun the biggest barrel in the forest; that they would find the militia down by the river; that they would chat uneventfully with its leaders, trying to con-firm the guess that the faction might be ready to come out of the bush and out from the war; and that he would then report back to British high command.

Despite his statement of the training goal, Marshall did not seem an arrogant man. He never stood exuberantly above the Sierra Leoneans, bellowing "Listennnnn to me!" Padded in the middle and mild in manner, he'd approached me three weeks before he was taken hostage: "Can I ask you a favor?" We sat in the mess tent at the training base. "Can I ask you a question?"

The padding wasn't enough to make him fat, but it softened his face as well, and amidst the lean strength of his men it gave him a look that was thoughtful, vulnerable. "Sure," I said.

"Have any of the guys said anything to you?" With his camouflage sleeve he blotted sweat from his thinning hair. "You know, used any words? Called the trainees anything, any names—called them flops?"

As in flip-flops, I realized, after a moment's pause.

"Because they shouldn't. I've talked to them about that. I don't want any of that."

And I still believe he was honestly troubled, concerned about more than bad publicity. But the way he steered, impromptu, into the West Side Boys' territory expressed a disdain for local warfare that went as deep as "flops" implied: The faction might number 300, but his eleven men could handle whatever came up.

"They go into the area of eagle like a common fowl," C. O. Gullit, an ex–West Side Boys leader, analyzed the British misjudgment, with nostalgic pride in his former troops. Near the river, Marshall and his men were surrounded so swiftly and adeptly—by about thirty of the militia, their largest gun dwarfed by Marshall's Browning—that they had to give up their weapons and vehicles without a fight. British self-certainty had accomplished the kind of surrender that had seemed the exclusive right of U.N. incompetence.

The eleven were held in a waterside village called Gberi Bana, ensconced between a span of pale green marsh and a wall of deep green palms. Writing on a mud wall read, "Dark Angel West Side Niggaz"; a totem, a red sphere with white fringe, dangled near the dungeon; the dungeon itself, a hand-dug oven six feet deep with a ceiling of barbed zinc, lay directly outside a colonial remnant of wooden doors and crumbled rooms. There the men were locked down, while the militia's commanders,

among them a Colonel Cambodia, sent out their requirements
for the hostages' release: the end of Kabbah's presidency and
freedom for their imprisoned leader, Brigadier Bomb Blast.

What exactly happened to Marshall and his team in Gberi
Bana is unclear. Later, the Ministry of Defense would confirm
that Marshall was beaten, that "mock executions" were held.
Men I knew from his regiment added details: He'd been blind-
folded and bound to a post, guns fired past his head. But the
hostages themselves have kept their public silence, as though to
describe their terror would dissolve the image of invincibility the
British quickly restored.

Five of the lowest ranking hostages were released for the
price of a single satellite phone. Negotiations stalled after that,
but the phone became a way to keep communication and trans-
mit coded messages to and from the captives. At dawn on the
seventeenth day, five U.K. helicopters and 150 commandos—
paratroopers descending ropes through the air and frogmen
crossing the river underwater—let loose a torrential barrage, a
paralyzing storm of explosions, on both the village and the
West Side Boys' main base on the opposite bank. The hostages,
prepped for the assault by code, were plucked safely onto the
choppers within minutes. Within two hours, the militia was all
but annihilated, killed or captured or scattered over the surrounding territory, which the British dispatched Neall Ellis to
cover with his gunship that morning, and for several days afterward, telling him, as he said, to "clean up" anyone he saw, that
there were no civilians in the area, only the fleeing enemy.

Even in their triumphant rescue, the British had been over-
confident. The militia hadn't quite adhered to the white vision
of local combat: "First there's firing and then everyone runs . . ."
They'd kept up their fire a good deal longer than expected,
hadn't run so soon as they were supposed to. One U.K. soldier
had been killed, twelve more wounded. Yet the British claimed
they were as confident as ever. Weeks earlier, I'd asked among
their top command what would happen if the troops ever took

casualties, whether public outcry back home would end a mission where no vital U.K. interests were at stake. "The public would want us to stay," I'd been told. "They'd want us to sort it out." And now, though there were minor cries from home to recall the troops, and warnings of "mission creep" from the prime minister's opponents, the high command proclaimed that it was "ramping up." With more government deserters now reversing themselves, abandoning their volatile alliance with the rebels, declaring themselves pro-government again, and flocking in for British instruction, the U.K. expanded the training of soldiers (increased the number from an initial core of 3,000 to 6,000 and later to 13,000; added officers' courses and specialty skills), sent trucks and mortars to support them, "guided" the freshly taught troops in a final mopping-up of the West Side Boys, staged mock attacks with U.K. paratroopers on the Freetown beaches, blasted warning rhythms of artillery from a warship offshore, and announced the creation of a 5,000-man rapid reaction force on constant standby, specially designated for Sierra Leone, ready to rush in if the country's fledgling democracy should need major protection.

The British talked more and more loudly of sending the new Sierra Leone Army to rout the R.U.F. from the half of the country it occupied; they talked more and more emphatically as if the army was sufficiently prepared. Foday Sankoh was by then a joint British and Sierra Leonean government prisoner, held in a secret location. (This hadn't been a British achievement—he'd been seized by a mob in the capital back in May, during the shattering of the last accord, after his men had opened fire on demonstrators outside his house, killing twenty-one—but that it had occurred after the British arrival, that he'd been handed over to the British, and that the British were party to his invisible imprisonment, his near-vanishing, only added to their reputation.) A pair of Sankoh henchmen, Issa Sesay and Gibril Massaquoi, had taken over in his absence, honor, and spirit. The R.U.F.'s brutality hadn't suffered (just as it hadn't suffered during a previous phase of the war, when Sankoh had been seized and confined, before being released). But now, with the West Side Boys so swiftly obliterated and especially with the British alluding heavily to their rapid reaction force, their mini-army looming in some form and "over the horizon" position they refused to specify, the R.U.F. seemed to take the British talk for fact, seemed to believe that onslaught was coming and that the balance of power had shifted monumentally.

In November 2000 the R.U.F. signed a cease-fire. The British were not the only factor. From over the border, Guinea had launched a series of helicopter assaults on rebel strongholds. And in Liberia, President Charles Taylor, broker for smuggled diamonds and illicit arms, had come under international pressure, and seemed a less reliable ally for the R.U.F. Yet the U.K. intervention had made by far the greatest difference. There were still the beginnings of a functional democratic society to be built. But if the truce held, if it led to the rebels actually ceding their land and their diamond mines and agreeing to a meaningful accord, if this time peace lasted, then, at the very least, the British had ended a decade of gruesome civil war. And they had held out hope for Western engagement on a war-wracked continent, a continent of implosion, the West had given up on.

NINE

Komba mounted a flight of wooden stairs; he climbed toward his first confession. The priest waited not in a booth, not in a church. He sat on a veranda, breeze drifting across the rail, trees in the yard shivering and sibilant. The generator had been shut off hours ago. The priest leaned back behind his small square table, smoking by candlelight. Komba reached the top of the stairs and saw, at the long veranda's far end, Father Chema alone: the full dark beard, the fine pointed nose, the slouch, the soft clothes, the slender arm dangling over the rail, the fingers flicking ashes. None of the other boys hovered around him. No one was lined up, hoping to talk. And the ones who sometimes slept, curled like dogs, on the verandah floor just outside Chema's room, or on the floor just inside, were nowhere in sight. It seemed the father was waiting only for him, had set aside this night specially for him, to pray as Komba longed to hear him pray: "For me life na come out good."

On his bedside table the Spanish priest kept a broken crucifix, a wooden statue missing its feet and arms. He'd found it in Italy, as he cleared decrepit furniture and sorted through forgotten books in an old house belonging to his order, the Xaverians. That had been years and years ago, before he'd ever heard of Sierra Leone, before the war. He had only just set out to become ordained. He had saved the shattered figure rather than tossing it away because it seemed to him beautiful, its dull surface of mottled brown, its face that was far from beatific, with cheeks sunken and mouth drawn, the features of an old man. This Jesus, scarcely three inches tall, close to death but looking not at all close to being raised up, appeared utterly forsaken, without strength, and Chema had carried the carving with him ever since, packed it carefully when the Xaverians sent him here almost a decade ago, first to bring food to those fleeing into camps because of the war, and now to live among boys like Komba. He had seen what they had done, seen the villagers running without arms, been forced to run himself. "The children," he called them, always. Some hadn't yet turned nine.

The children were brought to Father Chema—to his rehabilitation center on the grounds of a sprawling and ramshackle beachfront hotel, abandoned by its Lebanese owner as fighting put an end to tourism; used as a base by coup-makers and later by Nigerian troops—after surrendering at the U.N.'s demobilization camps. Occasionally they had fled their militias; more often, as with Komba, the head of one faction or another had relinquished some of his boy-soldiers as a gesture of goodwill, a proof of legitimacy, a ploy in negotiations. Some were offered, plenty held back. When Komba was trucked to the hotel, when the truck parked by the sea, he felt sure that the government had arranged to load him and the other boys into a line of waiting canoes. Komba, who had no idea how to swim, would be paddled out into the ocean. He would be pitched overboard.

As Komba told me this, he smiled shyly, almost as though he was still terrified of being taken away and drowned. With his high flesh-softened cheekbones and delicate chin, he looked helpless, innocent. Yet what *could* the nation do with boys like him? It had thousands to cope with. Hadn't his growing up twisted him too far? He'd been killing since around the age of twelve. He claimed not to have done any amputating himself on Lamin's hillside—assuming he told the truth, what could a boy's mind do with all he had seen, all he had taken part in? His had been the shooting around Lamin, his the burning, his unit, his boys, commanders above him but he, too, in command. Think, now, of a teenager in your world. Could you ever trust that boy again? That child so poisoned? Would you even call him a child, as Chema did? Would it matter?

Komba didn't show a great deal of remorse with me. He told of a raid he and his boys had carried out for food-finding. There had been a man caring for a small child, and Komba had spared him, setting him free from the line of villagers who would be marched away at gunpoint, bearing looted goods to the West Side Boys' encampment. Later, Komba and his crew had raided the same village. The man had launched himself at Komba, trying to wrestle away his gun. This Komba felt as a betrayal. When his boys finally pinned the man down, Komba told them not to shoot. "I operate on him with me ax," he recalled the opening, the eating, as vindication.

He seemed to feel, with me, only a faint degree of shame, just enough so that he attributed his violence to the violence that had been done to him, when he'd been stabbed below the eye and kidnapped for a life that had then become normal. "I no want you to cross my name," he said, when I offered to change it. "They force me."

Was I missing a regret more acute? An overwhelming guilt kept invisibly deep? Was his fear of being drowned the outward sign of a feeling that he could never start again, that he was too monstrous to be remade, that the only thing to be done was drop him to the bottom of the sea?

And what about a boy like Daniel, whose story I heard from Koskel, one of Chema's Sierra Leonean caregivers at the center. With an ax, Daniel had told the caregiver, he'd removed the hands of his own father. The same with his mother, the same with several siblings and cousins. Then all were shot except his two youngest sisters. Daniel was instructed, by the rebels who held him at gunpoint, to leave the two little girls alone, not to cut their hands, so there could be no chance of their bleeding to death, so they could describe for everyone what had happened. "I tell you one thing," Koskel remembered Daniel saying, about the years that had followed with the rebels, "to kill, when once you have started, you feel you are highly committed with drugs. It's not drugs. Is the killing. That is the kind of mind you develop."

To plunge over a cliff was to make what had happened at the precipice irrelevant. It no longer mattered that you had been forced over the edge. You were falling, and the falling became your entire life. After hacking off your father's hands, after leaving him so powerless, what else could you do but exercise horrendous power; what else could you do, when you had so destroyed your personal world, except destroy the world in general? No drugs were needed; the boundaries of self were already blown apart; you were in ecstasy.

These were the boys Chema collected. The first group of sixty or so, who had arrived shortly before Komba, were greeted by a U.N. camera crew, there to commemorate the center's opening. By the end of the day, lenses and car keys had been stolen. And by the time Komba came, having brought his West Side Boys unit with him, the children were at war. Komba joined in. For their lost guns the boys substituted smuggled knives, broken bottles, kerosene poured over one another's clothes before they set each other aflame. A concrete wall divided part of the hotel grounds. While the surf spread over the white sand beach, packs crouched on opposite sides of the wall, flinging Molotov cocktails over the barrier.

But compared to the kind of war they'd waged half their lives, Chema seemed to view this as progress rather than repetition, a movement away rather than a movement back. A few of the oldest, a few who showed some measure of calm, he hired as security guards or as caregivers, the counselors who lived with the boys in the hotel bungalows. He called assemblies and, in an upstairs hall festooned with construction paper ringlets, lectured against fighting. He shouted, berated, threatened to send the boys away. In no way was he a physically imposing man. It was clear, beneath his loose T-shirts and billowy drawstring pants, that his middle-aged body had no more form than his clothes. Only his face had definition, power, the dark eyes never sliding away in doubt or trepidation.

And there were things in his favor. The boys were used to discipline. Their commanders had taught them. If they didn't follow orders they were shot, or tied FM, or lowered into the *jojo*, a circular pit, shoulder width in diameter, with walls of long thorns and a floor of broken glass. The punishment Chema threatened—to banish them—rivaled those. Having been sent away from their armies, the boys felt stranded, like a species plucked from its habitat. What they'd known had been taken from them; what they had—all they had—was the sleeping mats in the bungalows, the regular meals, the classes in reading or, for those who felt they were too old, the lessons in carpentry, the afternoon games of soccer, the assemblies with Chema's scolding, his warnings. They had his parenting. He stood in for the fathers they had killed, the commanders they had followed.

So, for many of the teenagers who'd finished their live-in months at the center, and who Chema had placed in apprenticeships in the capital an hour's drive away, the need to be in his presence brought them back on frequent evenings to sleep on the floor outside his room. They had beds of their own, rooms Chema rented them near the carpentry shops and tailor's stalls where they trained. But they chose to curl directly on the floor of ragged blue-painted wood, to stay close, as Chema lowered himself onto his own narrow bed in his sliver of private space, behind a curtain of African cloth.

Only once had a boy reenacted his old ways against the priest himself, getting hold of an ax and coming at Chema, weapon raised. Others disarmed him before he brought the ax down.

Chema was more threatened by the village across the road. The people there felt no sympathy at all for the priest's children, given what the villagers had suffered from young soldiers like them. As a feud developed between the village and the center, sporadic fights led, one day, to Chema being surrounded as he walked along the road. Jabbing and flailing cutlasses in the air, the villagers seemed ready to take him hostage. His boys responded with rocks and with blades of their own. He was rescued by the violence of those whose aggression he hoped to purge.

When he told me of Komba's confession, Chema and I sat on the second-floor veranda, much as he had sat with Komba—late, the bungalows hushed with sleeping boys, the breeze gentle, the surf, on the opposite side of the main building, like the lightest of cymbals above the whisper of the mammoth trees. It hadn't been a confession in any formal Catholic sense. That never happened at the center. It had only been talking, confiding, spilling out, as the boys liked to do.

"Normally at night I sit here," he said, voice as soothing as all around us. "Normally at night, after they watch a video or have their activities, they come to sit with me. They talk about the day, what they have done in the war, anything. But I remember very well about Komba. I remember he had on a white T-shirt and short jeans trousers. I remember he wore this kind of hat, this cotton hat with a little rim. I don't remember the color but I remember at one moment he took it off and put it on the table. I remember very well because he was the first one to tell me about eating human beings. It was very difficult for me to listen. Now I can say I am a bit used to it. Other children come in with the same story. Drinking blood from their own hands, cutting the hands, over and over, it is part of the way. He cried little by little. And then he couldn't control himself. You see how strong he is, how proud he is. But he cried like a baby, sobbing, and I was shaking, trying not to cry.

"I know I have to control myself just to give confidence to the child. I was shaking, but I went around the table and held his head, scratching the back of his head. 'You no for worry.' That is what I told him. 'You go do fine. You done tell me what you done do. You no do bad. They force you to do it. You no do bad. They force you.' "

For that was the way Komba had related it, that he had not been a commander at the time. He had told about the Nigerian. There were other differences between the version Komba recounted to me and the confession he made to the priest, but that was the most crucial, the possible lie, the displacement of blame that, along with the convulsive tears, spoke of deep-rooted shame and guilt and regret. Either his commanders had ordered him to slice open the Nigerian, or he himself had been the one in charge, and had ordered his boys to hold the Nigerian down. I never got the chance to ask Komba why he gave different accounts, but Chema, that night of the confession, saw Komba and the Nigerian as equal victims. And after standing behind the boy and letting him cry with a hand rubbing and scratching and stroking the base of his scalp, after letting him sob and sob until the agony diminished while Chema delivered a soft semi-chant of reassurance, the father walked the child to his bungalow. There, the priest chatted quietly outside with two other boys while Komba washed at the pump and went in to sleep. The chatting was meant as comfort: to give Komba the feeling that all was undisturbed, ordinary, so that he wouldn't perceive what he'd confided as unmanageable, as cataclysmic. Then Chema walked back along the beachfront path.

And everything *was* ordinary. The waves rolled up the steep shore, playing the same rhythm they had played for all time. The moon cast its swath of turquoise across the ocean, the same light as the last month and the thousands of months before that and all the months before months existed. But Chema was trembling again, just trying to make it back to the main building, thirty yards, and up the flight of stairs and along the veranda, forty feet.

"I came back and I sat here at the table again by myself. It was dark, and I was trying to put in order my thoughts. And I couldn't. I have pictures, images. Of the Nigerian, this young

man. The picture of this young man's family in Nigeria, waiting
for him to come back. He was another victim in innocence. His
government sent him here for what? And his face—the face I saw
on his body is Komba's face. The body is Komba's. It was Komba
standing over him and Komba also lying there, pleading for his
life. Komba was receiving that wound. And I said, 'God, where
the hell were you at that moment?' My hands were shaking.
'God, the savior of humanity, protector of widows and orphans,
where the hell were you?'

"I don't know. My relationship with God is a very strange relationship. I get mad at Him many times for this kind of thing.
In the last year, so many times. 'God, where? Where? Where?'
And maybe I get no answer. Maybe the answer is, Where were
you? Where was I? What was *I* doing?"

It was, he explained, the meaning of the crucifix he had
saved long ago, knowing little, then, of meaning and nothing of
this place or what would happen here—knowing only the
statue's beauty.

"You are the hands and legs of Jesus. He cannot do anything
if you do not do it for him. Maybe that is the answer I got. He is
there and cannot do anything. But what am I doing, for Him, to
prevent innocent people from suffering?"

The crucifix held beauty and the crucifix held an answer.
But it offered no solace. Behind the blue curtain, beside the narrow bed where Chema slept, it lay on the end table between a
can of mosquito repellent and the worn pages of a Sunday
missal. But it could not calm him on that night of Komba's confession, when he did not sleep, when his mind veered between
'Where the hell were you?' and the traditional plea, 'God, give
me strength . . . ' It could not give him that. Strength had to
come from him. The crucifix begged of him, prayed to him, You
give *Me* strength, you *be* My strength . . . and soon, as the stories
like Komba's accumulated, his nightmares were filled with children raping, children cutting, children killing their mothers,
their fathers, and he: "It's a kind of impotence. You see these

things. They are happening right around me in my dream. You
cannot do anything."

He woke in the damp, hot, pitch dark room, the limbless
crucifix inches from his head.

The center's program was not elaborate. The caregivers, with
scant training in therapy of any kind, worked to keep order and
provide the boys an extra place for confiding besides the father's
veranda. Koskel was not a former soldier like a few of the others,
but a former student at the national university. He wore a T-shirt
bearing the face of the martial arts movie star Jean-Claude Van
Damme and in the evenings pumped iron with a weight set fashioned from rusty machine parts, scavenged axels and gears. He
injected himself with whatever muscle amassing chemicals he
could buy in the capital's pharmacies. His torso formed a V and
the Van Damme T-shirt was a second skin around his biceps; he
seemed the least likely therapist in any hemisphere. But the boys
came to him at the weight pile; the confiding began there. His
sister had been killed by the rebels. His father's house had been
burnt down. "If we don't help these people our society will descend," he said, "only descend. Of course we can forgive."

"I try to keep them occupied," he explained. "With the
classes, with sports. I try to help them forget. And at the end
of the day they will just lie down and sleep. And they will wake
up fresh."

Some of the boys stayed no longer than several weeks. The
goal was to find their families, reunite them with parents or relatives. But often there was no finding anyone, and sometimes
those who were found refused to take the children back. Certain
things were not forgiven.

For the refused, for all the orphans, there was a home until
they could, in some way, be restored into society. There were
math classes, one where I watched a boy named Mohammed, a
fourteen-year-old who said he'd never been to school at all, solve

geometry problems, solve algebraic equations. He had deformed
hands, extra half-pinkies extending from his thumbs. He'd been
taken by the R.U.F. around the age of six; in the jungle, between
raids, an older boy had taught him reading and writing and
math. Now, when he was called to the blackboard to solve for
variables, his handwriting was exquisite, with curls at the tips of
his Xs. His answers were perfect.

In the afternoons there was splashing in the ocean for those
not too scared of the sea. In the evenings there were videos in
the assembly hall, not the Chuck Norris and Rambo movies the
children requested but, in compromise with Chema, a compila-
tion of Michael Jackson music videos or a series of Nigerian soap
operas, or, what Chema preferred, films like *Free Willy*, with its
tale of a kidnapped whale returned to his family and a bitter or-
phan boy who finds a new home.

Each night Chema waited on the veranda. From the stories
the boys entrusted he did not try to convert them. On Sundays
they could attend the church down the road where he presided
or the Pentecostal church nearby—they went, the father said
without illusion, "just for something to do." On Fridays he offered them rides to a mosque. "To me," he said, "I feel I have
been sent by Jesus, if you want to talk that way, to Sierra Leone,
not to convert people, not to baptize people, to make Catholics,
no. I feel I have been sent here to do my best for the children, to
give the best of myself, to listen. That is what I do best. To listen."

The smaller ones had, too, a mother. Sister Adriana, a short
Italian in a blue smock, with a bush of dark hair and strong,
almost masculine hands, cooked for Chema and kissed the
youngest children goodnight. She ran the center's drug dispensary, made sure the children took their medicines, for TB, for
syphilis. And she tried, by coaxing the children to talk, "to take
the poison out."

She and six other nuns had been kidnapped by the R.U.F.
five years earlier. They'd seized her up north where she and the
others had been running a polio clinic and school. They held

her two months, marched her through the jungle, made her stare at the head of Robert Mackenzie, an American mercenary the government had hired before Neall. "So much seemed unreal," Adriana said, recalling Mackenzie's head on the post, the Nigerian bombs exploding near the rebels' base, the absence of clear demands that might end her captivity, the complete lack of control she felt over her own fate. "It's like a window opened up on the reality of life for people here. It's like the shutters opened. I am white. Always I have things to give, things to survive. But then I could only receive. A beggar. I could only hope to survive. I could do nothing, nothing."

Sometimes she spoke with disdain of the society that had as little—"nothing," she said over and over and over—as she had during those months. "Where is their dignity?" she asked, thinking of how frequently the older boys returned to the center, after they'd been placed in rented rooms and apprenticeships at the center's expense, to demand more money. She railed that they expected so little of themselves, that the country expected so little of itself, made no attempt to turn *itself* around, that everyone waited for rescue from outside. Yet her kidnapping had not only opened an emotional window on the nation's helplessness, it had opened her heart to her captors. "Between us, something," she remembered, interlocking the forefingers of her thick, powerful hands. She laughed at herself for thinking affectionately of the rebels who'd kept her, yet there had been, she was sure, affection on their part as well. Gibril Massaquoi, Sankoh's henchman, still referred to the seven nuns as "my sisters," she said, smiling.

Above all, her time as a captive, the months of helplessness, had united her with her mission, her vows of poverty, obedience. She had thought constantly of the parable of the rich young man in Luke. It held the line everyone knows: "It is easier for a camel to pass through the eye of a needle than for a rich man to enter the kingdom of heaven." To relinquish everything was the blessed state. But she had known this, before, only in her mind.

Now, in the jungle, she submitted. " 'Yes,' " she recalled saying again and again to herself, weeping. " 'Yes. Take it. Take it. It's nothing.' " She had never before given her life to God so fully. "It was very liberating." She was nearly in tears as she told me. "It was an appeal, a call to me as a woman. Adriana is a woman! My generosity, my everything was connected to God."

"Now the window has shut," she said—the window on under-standing, on empathy, on submission. She had, once more, everything she could need. She cooked fresh fish caught off the beach and drank bottled water to be sure she didn't become sick. She slept on a bed above the sea, lived in a way at once as-cetic and, by the standards of the country around her, luxuriant. She was, she felt, cut off from the country. But she was tied to this place by the blessing she had received here, when she had been seized. She wasn't going to come any closer to Jesus than she felt in Sierra Leone.

"It is no natural way of living," Chema spoke of his existence. Kept at a distance from the culture around him by the color of his skin—"people come to you saying I am your friend but they are always trying to get something"—and from the world by the priesthood—"there are many times," he said, "I feel lonely." A fleeting painful laugh came with this acknowledgment. "But it's the way I have chosen."

The choice had been made slowly. There had been, once, a girlfriend he'd met on a summer job, an archeological dig. There had been, during college in Spain, the weekends they'd spent volunteering. There had been her wish to do something else with their time together, his to do more for the prisoners, the gypsies. He had never been devoutly religious, hadn't at-tended Catholic school, but the religious orders could send him out into a world of need, could immerse him in a way no other volunteering could, could make such service his life. His parents had objected; his girlfriend had tried to sway him back. "And it's true that during the first years, if I was having problems or feeling down, I would call her. I was trying to trick myself: *Okay, if this doesn't work you can go back to her.* Then, little by little, I committed myself. The final vows. Ordination. You don't need it anymore," he said of the relationship he'd once had, the intimacies of romance, of sex. "At the beginning it is like something at the back of your head." His hand flicked gently at the air near the base of his skull. "But then it is like a ghost. It is gone."

Or not quite gone: "There are temptations. Human feelings. You don't have somebody who can share your life. I am alone. You go home, you go to your room, and that's it. But what you are doing, you can do it better the way you do it. Because it is everything. It's not work for me. It's not a job that I do." There were others, in the secular world of international aid, who tried to help child soldiers as he did. Just as there were those—with Doctors Without Borders, with the U.N.'s World Food Program—who opened clinics, who fed the displaced and the amputees. The people running such operations tended to cycle in and out of the country, in and out of the work, and to live among themselves. "We meet, we plan together, we think together," Chema said. "But for them, it is not their life. At five o'clock they go out. For me, this is all I have."

What he had was the attempt to transform. Once, at his table on the veranda, a teenager named Kallay handed him a plastic bag with a coconut inside. The boys often brought him what gifts they could manage: a sack of mangoes, a bunch of cassava. Kallay's name among the other children was Killer, a blunt tribute he'd earned in the bush. At the center, he led others into the fighting that Chema waited out as much as controlled. Killer hadn't softened to the priest at all; he appeared on the veranda only to command that he be given new swimming trunks, a cassette player, whatever he felt Chema should supply. It was as though all the looting he'd done in the war he felt entitled to do here as well. So Chema was pleased when Killer set the coconut on the table, a sudden gesture that things might change. He thanked Killer and stepped into his office to place the gift on his desk. Then, inside the sack, he saw not a coconut but a human skull.

"He said it was the head of the first man he ever killed, in Kabala. It was a kind of juju to protect him. And he had taken a ring from this man, and he wore this ring. It was part of the juju. But one day he was swimming here at the center, and the ring got lost in the sea. So he said it was the devil in the water here, the devil that took the ring from him, and that it meant he doesn't have protection. The head has no power anymore. He was bringing it to me, asking me to pray for him, to pray for his protection, because he had all these people coming to him at night. All the people he had killed. These were the dreams he had.

"So I would put my hand on his head. It was a way of making him feel secure. And I would help him to pray. I would tell him to ask God for whatever he wanted to ask. I would keep my hand on his head and he would whisper all the things he had done, asking for protection, because he saw in his dreams that people wanted revenge.

"Then after that period of about a month of praying together, he started playing with the toys."

Chema had asked one of the center's staff to bury the skull in a field on the far side of the driveway. Meanwhile the ring and skull had been replaced among Killer's most treasured possessions by a set of miniature cars, a teddy bear. Toys were donated to the center now and then, sent from abroad. Killer slept with the bear on his bungalow mat, kept it close through his dreams. Through the days and evenings he pushed the three-inch cars on the beachfront wall, pushed them along the veranda's rail.

His regression to a second childhood, a childhood he'd almost certainly never had, was not unusual. Hassan, a fifteen-year-old I came to know, sold flip-flops to aid workers on the Freetown beach, a business Chema helped him to start after his months at the center. Hassan covered the walls of his room with

posters of rappers brandishing guns, but adorned his bed with a
stuffed panda. When I took his picture, he wanted to pose with
the black-and-white bear cradled in his arms.

But regression didn't guarantee new innocence. After
Chema had spoken to me several times of his success with Killer,
I went to track him down. Following his phase with the toy cars,
Chema had asked Killer what he would like to do when he left
the center. Killer wanted to learn to drive, then to own a taxi,
and the priest had arranged this, paying for lessons and buying
Killer an old car. But when I stepped into the maze of shanties—
four dozen homes all bearing the single address Chema had
given me—and asked to be shown his house, I was told to wait,
that someone would bring Killer to me. Killer never appeared,
not that night or all the others I returned. I was told later that
he'd been dealing drugs for soldiers in one of the U.N. battalions and, most recently, employing his taxi for armed robberies.
By the time I discovered which door was his, and knocked both
early morning and late at night, he had left the capital, where
there was some vague semblance of a police department, and
headed to one of the R.U.F. towns upcountry.

Komba, after his sobbing, his sitting with head bowed and
Chema scratching lightly, didn't take up toy cars. Nor did he
stop fighting. "He wanted to change," Chema said, "but he
couldn't. He didn't have a way. He knew what he had left behind
and he didn't know what he had in front of him, and he would
snap—over nothing, over stupid things, over a line at the water
pump. Violent, very violent . . . "

He went again to the veranda, not to confess but to recall:
One night he told of a soccer game the soldiers had played between battles, another night of raiding a rare herd of cattle and
feasting for a week. His talk was almost of the everyday, so that
sometimes Chema saw the ordinary teenager Komba might have
become, a boy whose smile broke wide when he felt understood,
when Chema, who didn't say much as he listened, gave his minimal responses, made his listening noises, repeated a bit of the

sentence Komba had just spoken—Komba needed only that, the mere sense that he was heard. "Eeeeeh, Father Chema," he would say, as though continually surprised to discover that another human being took any interest in the way he'd grown up.

After several months, at most, teenagers like Komba and Killer were sent out from the center and into society, though the priest did try to visit them regularly at their homes or apprenticeships. The print of the past on their minds may have guaranteed the terrible violence of the future. But here so much was taken for granted, so much, by necessity, accepted. And so many more needed a few months of the attention Chema offered.

When Komba said he wanted to become an auto mechanic, Chema found a garage boss who would take him as an apprentice. For a fee, the boss would train and feed him. Chema paid, too, for a shack where Komba could sleep. He did the same for one of the West Side Boys soldiers who'd fought alongside Komba and who remained Komba's closest friend. They, who had ravaged the nation together, would room together. He gave them a small budget for decorations. They taped up posters of Tupac and Notorious, others of a rapper named Cocaine Dealer Master P, a duo who called themselves Capone and Noriega, and a nameless hero with a pair of machetes crossed in front of his bulging pectorals. There were no stuffed panda bears in sight.

One night Komba and I went to a simple restaurant. On the way, he insisted on taking a detour, going to his house, and putting on his only pair of long pants, vaguely tan corduroys whose ribs were worn flat. At dinner—because if he could ever afford to eat out it was a bowl of rice on the side of the road—he was unsure how to handle the red plastic basket of chicken and chips set before him. The chicken was on the bone, and after watching him hesitate I suggested quietly that it would be fine to use his fingers, that everyone did. Maybe he didn't hear me. Maybe he didn't believe me. Maybe he didn't care what I said. With his knife and fork he cut delicately at the leg bone in the unsteady basket. It tipped and skidded, and the chips sprayed over his side of the white plastic table. He didn't know what to do with them. I didn't know how to help without embarrassing him. Sidelong, he eyed the spillage for about a minute. He tried to continue talking. In the end, swiftly but with extreme decorum, he held his paper napkin over his fingers and picked up the chips without ever allowing them to touch his skin. He wrapped them in the napkin, bent over in his chair, and set his shame under the table.

TEN "I get a bit upset," Neall said, "when I hear all these people talking about how this time the enemy is sincere about peace. I don't believe it."

After the November cease-fire, negotiations crept forward between scattered battles. Neall took pride in the chance that peace might come, in his defense of democracy. He talked often of "fighting on the right side." His gunship bombardments had held Kabbah's enemies away from Freetown back in May, then compounded their British-induced fear as he blitzed their strongholds upcountry. The cease-fire, though, was a troubling reward. It meant he was kept from combat.

"The thing is, I'm a fighter. It's in my blood. I'm a warrior. I've been a warrior all my life."

He'd tried other careers. In 1992, when he'd been "too aggressive for the changing politics of the Defense Force," he'd left the South African military for a life of fishing—"but I was a poor fisherman." He tried farming. "But I wasn't a farmer." He'd promised himself never to think of piloting helicopters again, vowed to cut that need from his life. But the farm was on the route to a military air base, and every time a Puma would fly close he'd hear "that throbbing, that beating, and a Puma is magic and *whaaam* it goes over you and it has a much faster blade noise and when it passes by it's a rushing noise, like a steam train, or not like that but it's got purpose, and anyway you hear this noise and you think, Gee, I should be there."

A pilot he knew had gone off as a mercenary, flying freelance for the Muslims in Bosnia. When the man called, Neall said goodbye to his wife and two sons, and followed him there. In '95, a company named Executive Outcomes brought him to Sierra Leone. Executive Outcomes was the second mercenary outfit hired by then-President Strasser. The first was a group of fifty Ghurkhas, formerly of the British army, led by the American whose head Sister Adriana had seen.

But Executive Outcomes was, in certain ways, something new. White soldiers of fortune had been supplementing chaos around Africa since the end of colonialism, when the Irishman "Mad Mike" Hoare had been recruited by the CIA to lead his private forces of Belgian, French, Rhodesian, and South African soldiers to fight the Cold War in the Congo. A few years later, some of Mad Mike's former troops had attempted to overthrow Joseph Mobutu, whom the CIA had helped put in place as Congolese president. That had set the trend: soldiers of fortune, on behalf of just about anyone, aiding insurrections from Benin to the Comoros Islands. Yet Executive Outcomes sold itself as something different than those wandering rogues, something other than "dogs of war." With office suites and boardrooms in Pretoria and London, with pens in breast pockets and glossy brochures to hand out (as well as lighters stamped with the company logo, a chessboard knight), and with a onetime South African military commander turned chief executive officer, it was a leader within a rising corporate phenomenon, the "private military company."

There were plenty of others. From offices in Virginia, Military Professional Resources, Inc., contracted by the U.S. government, sent soldiers to the Balkans. But they were there to train, maybe direct—Executive Outcomes was one of the few corporations rigged for outright battle. And what it accomplished in Sierra Leone—200 men, backed by a gunship and transport aircraft, nearly obliterating the R.U.F., driving the rebels to the bargaining table within months while suffering only two of its own soldiers killed—would stir an international debate by the late 1990s: With third-world civil wars proliferating in the absence of Cold War constraints; with the U.N.'s peacekeeping missions largely unsuccessful and wildly expensive (the Sierra Leone mission cost 600 million dollars per year, while Executive Outcomes had been paid about 25 million); why not have the U.N., or even first-world governments, hire mercenaries to establish peace in brutal war zones?

Easy irony didn't make it a comical question. And worries about taking sides in civil wars didn't make the suggestion unthinkable. Certain conflicts, it was fair to argue, just had to be stopped. As the head of one private military company wrote in a London *Times* commentary: "The media can be in a burning village or a refugee camp or a bombed city and get the pictures out immediately. Most of the people watching CNN or Newsnight will have the same reaction: 'This is terrible. Something must be done.' But when they are invited to send their husbands or sons or daughters or pay for the operation out of their pounds, dollars or francs things are a little different: they want something done but they want someone else to do it. It's not so much that we can do things better than sovereign governments—though sometimes in Africa a heavy machine gun can be as effective as ten tanks elsewhere—it's that we can do it without any of the spin-offs that make military intervention unpalatable to governments; casualties among private military companies do not have the same emotive impact as those from national forces. And we can act quickly. Too often politicians won't make a decision to intervene either at all, or until it is too late."

But Executive Outcomes was quickly gone from Sierra Leone. International donors did not like to see their aid money funneled to mercenaries; it was hard not to believe that soldiers should kill for ideals rather than cash. There was also strong international suspicion that Executive Outcomes had negotiated additional pay in the form of future diamond concessions. And then, Foday Sankoh made the departure of Executive Outcomes a central part of an accord he signed in '96. Getting what he wanted, he went back to war.

Neall had been hired by Executive Outcomes toward the end of its combat role; next he went freelance to Zaire, once known as the Congo. There, the American-backed tyranny of President Mobutu was three decades old, and he'd long ago extended his name to Mobutu Sese Seko Kuku Ngbendu waza Banga, or "the all-powerful warrior who, because of his endurance and inflexible will to win, will go from conquest to conquest leaving fire in his wake." But Mobutu was beyond endurance. He commissioned Neall, met him in the presidential hometown of Gbadolite, swore him to loyalty, and had to flee the country before he could find Neall a gunship and a fuel supply to fight with.

With Mobutu gone, government soldiers stepped up their looting. They shot into the house where Neall and his two partners were stranded. The gunfight was a standoff, and later the three whites, hoping to pass themselves off as pilots for Air Zaire, left their guns behind and started hiking for the border twenty miles away. Every few hundred yards in town, troops stopped them, took an item or two—a watch, a pair of binoculars—or a large chunk of cash, and let them proceed. At a checkpoint at the town's edge, a group of four or five soldiers, one with a baby baboon on his shoulder, stripped them to their underwear—or, in Neall's case, to nothing, because he wasn't wearing any underwear. They took what possessions the men had left, permitted them to dress, allowed them, after some pleading, to keep their boots, and let one of them go. The soldiers ordered the two others, the ones who sounded South African, to put their hands on their heads and begin walking down the road. Civilians were looking on, a woman yelling at the troops, who were drunk, stoned. Neall knew the soldiers were now a firing squad, and couldn't explain, thinking back, why he hadn't tried to run. "I don't know. Because there were too many of them for a start, and we were too close. And we'd had a few brushes with these people, you know, been beaten. Gun butts, shot at. One of us lost ten thousand dollars. I'd lost thirteen hundred, and the other guy about five or six, you know what I mean? Psychologically," he laughed for half a second, "we were a bit down."

So they walked away from the squad with their hands on their heads. "The mind's a blank. You know you're going to die, and I was praying, God I'm okay, don't be too harsh. But actually you're quite numb."

At about twenty yards they obeyed another order: They turned around. The squad fired. They fired and fired, dozens of rounds it seemed, and missed and missed. The woman kept yelling, taunting, distracting, unhappy with the soldiers for myriad other reasons. They pointed their guns toward her. At last, the mercenaries ran. A government officer took pity on them, hid them, had his son guide them to the border.

The experience made him rethink his chosen profession. "But when you're sitting at home doing nothing and nothing seems to be working out . . ." Outside Capetown, he wandered the edges of a mountainside farm, sleeping in the bush as a *bucchu wagter*, a lone security guard making sure no one stole the *bucchu* plants—the source of a popular homeopathic remedy for bladder infections.

By '98 he was back in Sierra Leone. He was hired first by another private military company; when the company left, he fought on his own. He headed his own miniature air force, the only air force Kabbah's government had, comprised of one transport helicopter and one MI-24 gunship. He employed (depending on need and availability) another pilot from South Africa, a doorgunner known as Fred the Fijian (who was almost as famous as Neall, on account of his high-skilled strafing as well as the training camp he'd led for hunting society forces), an Ethiopian flight engineer, and two local gunners who had, quite recently, helped to chase out the president they now fought for. Neall was paid by the government (with precisely whose aid money it was difficult to say), and though Kabbah's democracy might well have been dead without him, he still found himself kicking back bribes to Kabbah's uncontrolled ministers and bureaucrats. He said he factored in 10 to 15 percent of his income for this expense, to be sure his payments came through.

As for other compensation—the sort of concessions Executive Outcomes had been accused of commanding—it seemed pretty clear that Neall didn't operate on a grand scale. He invested a bit in a miner named Lou, a skinny Vietnam vet from Las Vegas who wore a gold chain and a stiff black toupee that looked less like hair than a baseball cap worn backward. Lou had been around Sierra Leone since '95, predicting riches like Rhodes had known. When I went to track him down upcountry, he was living in a shed whose greatest luxury was an unflushing toilet long filling with waste. Now he planned to switch from diamonds to gold. Gold, he declared, was certain. He knew a man, knew him personally, he insisted, who'd made eighty-one million in five months, then disappeared, leaving his machines to rust in the jungle. "Just left them and walked away. He didn't care. He had his money. That's the kind of money I'm talking about." (About the array of hapless lode hunters who washed out in Sierra Leone, Mike Kpukumu's American partner, who'd sunk cash into Lou's mining before trying to import fertilizer, was fond of saying, "It took me a while to find out, but diamonds don't grow on trees and gold doesn't sprout from the ground.")

No, Neall hadn't been developing any fortune. What he'd been doing, Christmas Day of '98, was loading the transport chopper with ammunition and flying it to the last government troops still fighting for Kabbah in the northern town of Makeni. As he landed, the town's helipad was deserted. The troops didn't want to stand exposed with rebel RPGs exploding in the trees nearby. They didn't want to unload. Two and a half tons of ammunition in its bay, the chopper was now grounded, the helipad too small for the running start Neall needed to take off with so much cargo. His crew began unloading: two men, endless crates. The rebels started finding their range; the explosions edged closer. Wanting to be gone the instant the MI-17 was light enough, Neall stayed strapped in, perched above the ground in a glass bubble, tank half-filled with fuel, waiting for an RPG to ignite his own inferno. And when he finally got into the air, he couldn't push the machine past half speed. The bay was overloaded with escaping troops who'd dived in at the last second.

They were hanging from the rear doors, which in the panic no one had shut. As Neall landed again in government territory, a soldier and his door, snapped off in the rotor gust, came rocketing past the cockpit.

And what he'd been doing, in May 2000, was climbing into his MI-24, climbing nimbly by awkward toeholds, then swinging himself in, this stocky man in a green jumpsuit. (With the same aircraft, a year earlier, he'd been told to shoot down a Red Cross helicopter that the Nigerians and Neall believed was supplying the rebels. Had the Red Cross flown a certain route that day, a route both the Nigerians and Neall felt would prove their suspicions, the relief workers would have been incinerated.) Usually he flew low, kept enemy aim blocked by the trees, kept them blind until he bore down on them, used the foliage to muffle the sound of his approach, but in early May he stayed high over the road leading to Freetown, made himself visible. He wanted to be shot at. The enemy was near the capital, and this was the best way to pinpoint their heavy weapons. Get fired at; fire back. You had to take your chances. "The biggest and best game . . . the greatest game available . . . you know, the stakes are so high . . . if you win, you win; if you lose . . . " It was a technique he'd used before. "You try to switch off. You don't think. You concentrate on the job. If you start thinking about what might be there for you . . ." Sometimes his leg began twitching in the cockpit. He pounded his thigh to make it quit jumping.

No one told him to fly this way. The British would later question it, wishing he wouldn't put the gunship at such risk. But though, at different stages, the Nigerians and the British directed him, no one exactly controlled him. He devised his own missions, his own methods, tried to believe "I don't do a suicidal thing, I don't have a suicidal tendency." He placed his faith in the chopper's armored plating that protected him to some degree, and in his own quick reactions, though the MI-24 was prone to rolling over and the sudden steep banking he had to perform put him way outside the guidelines.

In the cockpit's tight shell, the controls to the arsenal were inches from his shins. The little steel switches were marked with a label-maker—the labels like the kind I'd put on notebooks as a kid. The baby blue tabs with raised white lettering said "rocket burst" and "bombs launch" and "MG burst" and gave Neall the choice of fixing the Gatling gun's eruption to "short" or "medium" or "long." Once he set the munitions panel, once he looked away from those child-like tabs, everything happened from the black cyclic stick between his legs. The steering was there, and the brake, and the black button at the tip.

The switches were set before the final approach. Then, with a flick of the button's cover and a one-finger jab of pressure, a force less than you would use for a push-button phone, the chopper's entire arsenal—guns, bombs, rockets—was unleashed at once, twenty seconds of localized apocalypse.

But almost always there were problems. The warning panel lit bright red on nearly every flight. Since the gunship was Russian made, and since the categories of warning were spelled out in Russian, Neall often just had to hope that the failure wasn't serious. (There was a translation card, but it wasn't the easiest thing to consult in the minutes before attack.) And then the guns tended to jam. Suddenly, in the midst of Armageddon, he would quit feeling their vibrations, the one-ton recoil; he would sense himself a bit less like a god swooping low in the sky, a bit more like a hang glider dangling naked. And on that May morning just before dawn, no matter how well the aircraft worked, on his flight up the road toward the enemy advance he was setting himself up to be shot down like a plump duck.

For two days he'd been flying that same vulnerable route, so the rebels would expect him. For two days he'd been waiting for them to haul out their heavy guns, expose them in their desire to take down the government's best weapon (and the pilot who, it was rumored, had a high price on his head). Now, speeding through the paling dark, he could see the swamp snaking west of the road, the half-sunken tugboats in the harbor, the mountains to the east, the corrugated roofs below. The tracer rounds came just before full sunrise, phosphorescent flames glowing green against a sky of faint pink and gray. They were gorgeous, those illuminated bullet-tails, and as long as he could see them it meant he was safe—the rounds were traveling under or over or in front of the helicopter. If the rebels found their aim, if the bullets came straight at the gunship, the tracers wouldn't be visible.

He spotted the 14.5 and 12.7 machine guns on trucks along the road. "Target visual," he told his crew. He rolled tight, banked hard, dived down, dozens of rebel soldiers running, scattering, looking from the air like "long swastikas," he thought, one arm and one leg bent and raised. He touched the black button. The gunship trembled, volcanic. Shrapnel dropped bodies without drama; the soldiers appeared simply to fall, as if tripped. "It's actually a bit of an anti-climax," Neall explained. He destroyed the trucks with their mounted guns. "It's not like the movies. When the rocket hits the vehicle there's no flash or cloud of smoke. Nothing shoots hundreds of feet into the air. I suppose if you hit the petrol tank it would be quite nice, but I've never had that privilege. You get a slight fire because there is some fuel around. And pieces start falling off the vehicle."

"If you can't take a joke," Neall muttered triumphantly in the cockpit, veering away from the rebel maimed, the rebel dead, "don't join the army."

Peace was difficult, personally. Thoughts that it might take hold led to thoughts that, at fifty, age was overtaking him, that his vision was going, his hearing, that soon he wouldn't be fit for combat if the fighting heated up again, or if he went to find some other war. Then what would he do? Go civil? Try fishing again? "Settle down on the ground while other people go up and have fun and shoot"?

"I'm going blind," he thought improbably. "I'm wearing

glasses . . . The senses start deteriorating . . . My awareness, my reactions . . . " How much longer would they be sharp enough for battle? "The thing is, I'm going to kill myself." He pictured misjudgments under fire that cost his life and the lives of his crew. The cease-fire left him too much time to think in general. It relegated him to reconnaissance and basic, uneventful transport, and to waiting, waiting. It was not healthy.

But it surely was for Michael. For the time being, he didn't have to think about the next time he'd need to put down his books and pick up his rifle and fight—and remove bullets and stitch spilling arteries near the battlefield—until there was a buffer around the capital, until he could run back to studying again. For the time being, he could take me to the lab of Freetown's main hospital, where he offered me the lone pair of rubber gloves.

They lay on the counter, amidst disease-ridden samples of stool and urine, mucus and blood. The stool sat within folded scraps of torn newspaper; the mucus was packaged the same way. The test tubes full of urine and blood had no stoppers, only bits of toilet paper stuffed into their necks. A good number of the samples would reveal tuberculosis, Michael had told me, which would mean the likelihood of AIDS. And I knew that two relief workers upcountry had lately died of Lassa fever. The disease was treatable only if diagnosed in the first several days, and for the first several days it masqueraded as nothing worse than a bad cold. Then the Ebola-like bleeding, the ballooning of the face and neck, the neurological dysfunction, could begin. For those who survived, one quarter wound up deaf.

I started persuading myself that I should have the gloves, though he would be working with the samples and I merely standing beside him to watch. Michael was used to a lack of safety, I was not. This was his world, not mine. My standards of self-protection were higher. My health, my life—this was what the logic came down to—were worth more than his. I wanted that latex between my hands and all the illness of his country, and had to believe, in this laboratory universe of impossibly limited resources, that his needs were less than my own.

"You have them," Michael said, holding the gloves toward me by the wrists.

The slack latex hands dangled between us.

I refused, barely.

He slipped the gloves over long, graceful fingers, slipped them on easily, the rubber gone limp from earlier use. Then he led me through the diagnostics he'd learned, partly in class but mostly in this room, where he spent many of his free hours, making himself an unpaid assistant to the rarely paid technician. "We're looking," Michael taught me, "for specific morphological characters."

In the room of bleary light and shadowed corners, three or four toothpicks lay, without wrapping, on the wooden counter. Taking one, he dabbed stool onto a chipped slide marked with an ancient strip of tape and the faint initials of some bygone patient. "Intestinal worms are of course extremely common in the region." He lectured precisely, confidently, quietly. "*Ascaris lumbricoides*—that is roundworm; *enterobius vermicularis*—that is pinworm; *taenia solium*—that is tapeworm . . ." He went on with his list, the Latin always first, as he set the slide on one of the lab's two functioning microscopes, a model that might have served sixth graders in the West. At our feet an open cardboard box, which had once held canned sardines, was the only receptacle for any medical detritus that existed in a lab where almost everything was reused. A small centrifuge was the lone working machine, its surface encrusted with dried urine and plasma but its motor capable of spinning, so long as there was electricity. Two or three days each week it went out for long periods, and the samples spoiled in the heat. "Can you see the lateral spine projecting from the ovum?" he asked, his speech an antidote to the conditions around us, when I took my turn at the eyepiece. "That is *shistosoma mansoni*."

Next, with thin-wristed hands as agile as his tongue, he reached for the blood and "mucoid substance" of a suspected TB case. In the unlit hallway outside the lab's open door, a half dozen patients or their relatives sat on a bench, awaiting results from the specimens they'd brought. They waited mutely, staring at the opposite wall of the tunnel-like corridor. They waited as though diagnosis, when it came, wouldn't matter. And it wouldn't, not much, not to most of them. In the hospital, bribes were often required and strikes were routine. On the wards, where patients had to buy even aspirin from the staff, failing bodies were attended by daughters or nieces who slept under the beds, lived under the beds. The girls had been sent by their families as makeshift nurses, condemned to spend their nights and days directly beneath the dying, some crouching silently behind colostomy bags.

Drugs were rarely used. To purge a simple case of worms cost a local fortune. The cheaper way—and the traditional way— was to buy a murky fluid from the "peppah doctor," his bowls and jars spread beside the road. "Drink till you belly full," the peppah doctor would prescribe between hawking similar beverages for all the maladies of mankind. The effect, Michael said, was little but a toxified gut. The worm ovum might be suppressed briefly; then it flourished again, blocking organs, bringing anemia. And the cure for TB was on the street as well. The difficulty had nothing to do with price. Foreign donors funded programs for the big-name diseases, but the medicine for TB turned the urine, and sometimes the sweat and saliva, red. The infected quit taking it in fear of devils.

With HIV, diagnosis was meaningless. It was denied, dismissed. Until the worst symptoms took hold, the illness wasn't inside. The people went on as before.

Delicately, Michael dipped a toothpick into the mucus and stretched a viscous and vividly green strand across a slide. I asked if he ever felt disheartened, given the situation he'd just outlined, if he ever felt that his work in the lab and in medical school might, in some ways, amount to nothing. He didn't glance up at my question. He remained focused, painting the specimen smoothly across the glass, spreading it even and thin, fingers lightly pincing the toothpick as though it were a specialized tool and the mucus something precious. "No," he answered. "I believe in evolution, not revolution. Rome wasn't built in a day." And the stock phrases would have been empty, elsewhere. But here the words carried strange weight, for it was possible to feel, in Sierra Leone, what it would take to transform a society, to build a new civilization. The immensity of the task was palpable. There must have been a relentless burden on the shoulders, a constant resistance to every step, for anyone who aimed at even a part of such change. My shoulders felt too weak, my lungs too shallow, to contemplate it.

He added a red dye to the slide, then needed to heat the specimen "in order to break down the lipid layer so the stain can penetrate the microbacterium." Elsewhere, this would have been accomplished by placing the slide for two hours inside an incubator set to 75 degrees Celsius. Here, Michael found on the counter the stub of a candle, an inch or two high. Lighting it, he lifted the flame, passing it back and forth beneath the glass. Like the toothpick, in his fingers the candle seemed a specialized tool. And in that place it seemed a beacon.

When Michael's father had died, Michael had just begun medical school and hadn't known enough to diagnose him. At a clinic the father was told he had pneumonia; he was coughing blood before anyone called his illness TB, and by then it was too late. "There are the culprits," Michael said to me now. "We have apprehended them." He drew me toward the microscope, showed me the scattered cells that meant TB. The electricity went down. The centrifuge quit spinning, quit thrumming. The lab's minimal light dimmed, coming only through the heavy curtains that did what they could to hold back the heat. Michael

went to a rack of three test tubes and spoke of "erythrocytic sed-
imentation," explaining the rate of the blood's separation as a
non-specific test for disease, before he talked of the bullets he'd
seen turned to water, the voices he'd heard speak from the
grave, the fingers grown long enough to encircle a man's body,
the rounds that had reversed course when a staff was pointed,
the soldiers who could make themselves vanish—all that he
knew from his time fighting with the Kamajors. "Listen to me,"
he said. "I have been in school. I do appreciate what I have
learned. I do cherish it so much and believe that it paves my way.
But Daniel, if you don't trust what the Kamajor claims, at least
appreciate what he can accomplish. Wonders have begun way
back in the Babylonian days. There, in Babylon, presently Iraq,
there was a hanging garden that defied the rules of science, the
principle of gravity. Plenty of wonders have passed on this earth
ever since, and the country for wonders, for this time, it is here.
I am a living witness. Certain things that have happened I will
never say. Certain things remain secret. I will tell you only what
you ought to know, otherwise I will be haunted. I will be pun-
ished by the spirits.

"I was doubting, like yourself, at first. When I was initiated I
was not willing to line up with the others and put myself in front
of the gun. But somebody shot at me while I was not aware, and
from that point onward I became more convinced. I have already told you about the bullet that struck my shoulder but dam-
aged only my jeans jacket. I have told you about the belt that
pulled tightly around my waist whenever an ambush was nearby.
Now think of the great father of modern science, Albert Ein-
stein. When he first proposed his theories, of course some people believed he was an imbecile. But his ideas would conquer.
His ideas would bring an empire to its knees. You will see the
same things here, with disease. Daniel, when I am ready I will
call you. From the other side of the world, you will come and be
my witness."

He stressed the distinction between the peppah doctors,

"the sellers of false medicines and waters that are poison," and the true priests, and I thought of Hinga Norman, the defense minister, who had told me of a new world age, when the high priests of Sierra Leone would be recognized as seers and prophets. They were just about to be discovered; the long delay had been caused by a combination of remoteness and the lack of a written record. Because their miracles had not been written down, they had been given no credibility in the West. "The prophets are here, but what is happening is that our size as a nation is small—maybe if you put the needle into ink and you just drop it onto the globe that is the size of us on the world. So we cannot shout loudly. Only when our knowledge will be written down. But the other thing is jealousy. The powerful men were jealous of Jesus's power to heal. But Jesus was heard."

And not so long into the future, in Michael's vision, Sierra Leone would be transformed. His voice lowered in the darkened lab. "The absolute cure for all cancers, for leukemia, for all the most dreadful tumors, for the most dreadful contagion, and by that I mean HIV, will come from here. Oh, Daniel, that is my dream. Through my work with the priests, my tests in the laboratory. I will publicize what these great men can accomplish with their powers. It will take time and dedication. But I will tell you for free, Sierra Leone will be a paradise. People will come from all over. The rich will come, the poor will come, the middle class will come. The hotels will be full. The hospitals will thrive. There will be such an economic boost, such a big economic boost, a boost you cannot imagine. And you will see me, I will be a rich man. Sierra Leone is a small country. Some do not know where Sierra Leone lies. But soon they will try to find where; desperately they will try. You know that when someone is in pain, the most severe pain, he will pay anything in order to be cured. Anything you ask him for. Oh, Daniel, it will be paradise."

ELEVEN I want to tell you the truth. And if I tell you that Michael's intelligence and will and Lamin's miraculous determination and Komba's wish for a different life filled me with a great sense of hope for Sierra Leone, then I am not dealing in the truth at all. During the year that followed the cease-fire, hope had only vaguely to do with what I felt. The agreement kept holding, tenuously. The rebels clung to their half of the country, clung to the best diamond mines, and there were skirmishes between them and the hunting societies. There were villages burned, mass abductions, people shot or mutilated, children slaughtered. But the outbreaks were brief. They were nothing terrible by the standards the country had grown to adopt, nothing the cease-fire couldn't absorb. There was talk—though the rebels would not relinquish their guns—of the R.U.F. becoming a political party. There was talk of national elections.

No, my despair didn't come from broken peace.

But before I say anything more, I must state the obvious, though I have stated it already. I am white. It needs saying because what I perceived in Sierra Leone may have so much to do with my color as to make whatever I tell you unreliable and irrelevant. In the end, I do not believe this. But I do wonder if it is true. I do wonder if another writer—a black writer, especially— would have seen the nation in some completely different way, if the reality I saw was a screen, blocking my view of what was real behind it. For at some deep level I cannot know, to a degree I cannot measure—a degree I can only hope was slight—I was drawn to Sierra Leone precisely because its terror and self-destruction offered me a kind of primal self-affirmation, a seductive proof, no matter how insidiously false, of the superiority of my own race.

When Captain Rosenfeld bellowed, "Listennnn to me!" and the black soldiers answered, "Listen to de white man!"; when the white man's mortars exploded in the hillside jungle and the blacks gave out their joyous, anachronistic cry, "Long live the British!"; when Foday spoke the psychology of a nation, explaining, "The black man witchcraft, it only for spoil . . . The white man witchcraft, you are making something to better the world," a part of me recoiled, felt hollowed out from witnessing such an absence of pride, such an embrace of the imperial past, felt weak from taking in a people's underlying self-hatred. But a smaller, covert part of me was exhilarated. Such scenes, such words, made me at once sick with sadness and faintly electrified. The pleasure turned on itself and added to the sickness, for it flooded me with self-disgust. It tempted me and ate away at me. But the pleasure was there, at least at the beginning. It was there—a vague excitement born of racial dominance—when I was with Neall, and there with the British out on patrol. I wish that when the bartender had rubbed his dark forearm and said, "It's in the skin," blaming his race for the failures of his nation, his continent, I had experienced only the urgent need to disagree. But that was not so.

One afternoon during my first trip to Sierra Leone, at the landing strip outside the mining town of Bo, a gray-bearded man in a white fez beckoned me aside. I stepped away from the pair of wrecked propeller planes that decorated the edges of the lone runway, and ducked into a side room of the bleak shed that served as the airport lounge. The man, with a leprechaun's impish smile, said he was a photographer, that he had some pictures he wanted to show me. From a vinyl shoulder bag he brought a little plastic album. On its cover, in a heart-shaped window, was a portrait of the movie star Tim Robbins, beaming in a beige tweed jacket and smooth white T-shirt.

The leprechaun in a safari suit handed me the booklet. I turned through the snapshots in their dusty sheaths: a severed head propped against pale stone; another on a stand of criss-crossed stakes; a third set directly on sandy ground; a fourth held aloft in a pair of hands, a celebratory crowd pressing near, touching and pointing at the scalp; a fifth—or a fifth and sixth, for there were two heads in the picture—teetering on a concrete block, the young boys' faces sleeping side by side, heads leaning against each other. I stared. A twelve-year-old inspecting Miss July couldn't have been more riveted. Trying not to appear too interested, I handed the album back.

My plane droned close then, and I was too ashamed to buy the pornography I wanted. But on my next trip to Bo I was more forthright. Amidst the shoddy storefronts of the Lebanese diamond dealers, the establishments named "Moon Diamond Office" and "Big Mac Diamond Office" and "Good Luck Diamond Office" whose garish, faded signs gave the faint impression of a run-down amusement park, I found the spry, smiling man in the hovel that was his studio. He showed me proudly the credentials he'd been given at various stages during the decade of war, the old letters from the Nigerians and the government army, allowing him to cover their campaigns. This picture, he said, of four men in civilian clothes posing with a bound and headless rebel body, had been taken after a government victory against the R.U.F. The men, one looking urbane in white slacks and a natty sportshirt, its boldly patterned fabric in fine condition, knelt to be sure they got in the frame. This one—I turned the pages slowly, and he leaned tight, explaining—he'd snapped away from battle, behind a Kamajor roadblock. Five hunting society soldiers, just stirred from a nap, lay on the patchy dirt and grass right beside the nude corpse of a man who'd upset them in some way at their checkpoint. The body had been chopped at a bit, and part of one leg was missing, but its limbs were otherwise attached, as was its head and penis. Apparently the soldiers had grown tired in the sun and stopped to doze, their arms and hands lolling indifferently against their victim, before they continued their mutilation.

We came to the heads. The one resting in the crotch of criss-crossed stakes belonged to a young, smooth-skinned rebel. The hand of a government soldier lay on the victim's hair, keeping the boy's head upright for the photographer. Another government soldier tried to crowd into the close-up, his sunglasses next to the head's slack mouth.

The one on sandy ground and the one held aloft were, it turned out, the same head, once belonging to an R.U.F. juju man and now displayed in two different ways by the government troops who'd captured him. In the first, the soldiers had composed a sort of still life: A detached forearm with an upturned palm lay a few inches from the long face with its closed eyes, the overall effect being, with listless thumb beside listless jaw, like a cubist portrait of sleep. The second arrangement was less artistic, just a cluster of well-pleased troops, teens with their gray-haired leader, smiling and pointing.

But the most striking display in the album was a hood ornament on a government captain's pickup. The rebel head, with its somewhat fatty face, wore Clark Kent eyeglasses and had the stub of a cigarette stuck between its lips. String was wrapped haphazardly but repeatedly around the trophy, denting the full cheeks and small ears, the soft chin and wide forehead, and binding the ornament, just above the Nissan name, to the top bar of the heavy all-terrain grill.

I bought the album for a hundred dollars, the first price the photographer asked. I could have followed the African tradition and bargained, getting it for thirty or twenty-five, but the extra money was an offering, a futile attempt to wipe away my guilt and discomfort. I wanted the snapshots for straightforward journalistic reasons, but I knew it wasn't only that. And later, staring, and thinking of how eagerly the soldiers had encouraged the photographer to memorialize their victories in these images, I was pulled toward conclusions about the culture I was dealing with, conclusions infused by race. Reminding myself that similar mutilations—less frequent but perhaps carried out with equal pride—had occurred in the Balkans, didn't have much effect on my thinking. Nor did all my knowledge of the Holocaust's mechanistic savagery that had wiped out most of my grandmother's family and whose scale made a quaint miniature of the brutality I was confronting. Those white episodes in the history of modern atrocity didn't eradicate the swarm of racist notions about *these* atrocities. The lesson, for me in Africa, of those white episodes, I knew already and had no trouble believing: We are all capable of apparently inconceivable acts; we are all capable of congratulating ourselves for them. But understanding this truth, even at the deepest levels of liberal faith, was not to eliminate a contradictory notion: that these acts, here, were especially primitive, barbaric, savage. The contradiction was irrelevant. Racism does not occupy the realm of logic. It lives beneath the level of reason. And no matter how reasonable I tried to be, no matter how clearly I tried to see the country I planned to write about, I know that the irrational tinted everything.

Still, Sierra Leone was what it was, and a great deal of Africa, despite all its Michaels and Lamins, wasn't much better. (Sudan neared a half century of civil war; Burundi and the Democratic Republic of the Congo kept up their internal fighting; Rwanda's staggering genocide was just in the past; and a dozen other conflicts simmered, from northern Uganda to the Central African Republic to the once-stable Ivory Coast, waiting to replace the conflagrations that might somehow die down before flaring again, waiting, on a continent with 10 percent of the world's population and 60 percent of its current civil war deaths, to make a fool of anyone, as Africa recently had, who declared that an era of progress was replacing its history of devastation.) And as I spent time in Sierra Leone after having traveled widely on the continent, it wasn't racist merely to feel oppressively aware of such vast self-ravaging. Were there explanations? Yes, there were, a swirl of answers:

The trans-Atlantic slave trade had done such violence, psychic as well as physical, that sub-Saharan Africa, black Africa, the Africa that appeared most implosive, had never recovered; the trans-Saharan slave trade, which took millions to the Arab north, had done almost as much damage; the landscape of Africa, with its impoverished soil even south of the Sahara, had kept population densities low from the beginning of history, limiting the early development of agricultural societies and thus retarding the advance of civilization (at least as civilization is known in Western terms); the overwhelming tropical diseases of Africa had engendered through millennia a continental zeitgeist of fatalism; the era of European imperialism hacked up the continent in ways that ignored ethnic boundaries and roped together tribes that couldn't possibly coexist when the colonies became nations, or, alternatively, the crime of colonialism had been not the binding together of rival tribes but the *creation* of tribal rivalries in order to ease European rule; the colonial governments had left a legacy of brutality that included, in the Congo of Belgium's King Leopold, encouraging the amputation of hands (cut from corpses by Congolese paramilitaries, then delivered to European overlords as proof that those villagers who hadn't produced enough rubber had been executed, that spent bullets had gone to good use); the colonial governments had chosen to promote the least capable African administrators and the most volatile military officers in order to prove that whites were, in fact, indispensable; the Cold War had propped up Africa's worst dictators and prevented the growth of functional nation-states; African "Big Men" and warlords manipulated ethnic distrust to mimic the absolute power of imperial rule; Western aid nurtured a continent of dependence and inertia; African traditions of communal values and land ownership had constrained individual identity and the creative use of economic capital and thus stunted material progress; the Cold War had flooded Africa with modern weapons; wretched poverty made warfare—chaotic, factionalized warfare marked by constant looting—an attractive means of self-support for African youth; the end of the Cold War had removed an overarching restraint and released the forces that rose toward millennial anarchy . . .

Some of the theories applied across the continent, some to sets of countries, and then there were the factors specific to Sierra Leone's annihilation, with its particular sadism, its mass amputations on civilians left alive, an unprecedented tactic with no clear source. There were the diamonds that bought arms and sparked battles to control the mines; the machinations and regional vendettas of Charles Taylor in neighboring Liberia; and a historic divide between the inland tribes and the descendants of the colony's nineteenth-century recaptives, a variation on the ethnic rivalries that were explosive elsewhere in Africa but a factor that was relatively minor here, so that the ancestral explanation that somehow soothed as well as horrified in the case of Rwanda—for at least Rwanda's genocide could be boxed with the basic label of tribal hatred, of lethal enmity for the Other—could not much serve for Sierra Leone, where the swirl of explanations left the feeling that there were no answers at all, that the stacks of books I read and tunnels of thinking I descended could never lead to understanding, that those who offered theses were either desperate or deceitful, determined to give coherence more than truth, that here, in this tiny sweltering wasteland saturated with rain and blood, all explanations were meaningless, powerless against the anger and revulsion, the blame and self-blame, the dizziness and depression of not-knowing.

As their mission reached and passed one year, and as they spoke of a five-year plan, the British stared at the likelihood of their own ultimate failure. They stared not only from the military but from the civilian side. Keith Biddle, the police chief from Kent, ever disheveled in his blue uniform, with long wisps of white hair flying from beneath his blue cap, had arrived two years before most of his countrymen. "Beam me up, Scotty," he sighed, dreaming at times of his own exit from futility, as he talked of the rule of law like a haze on some unreachable horizon. And Ian Russell, part of a British-run anti-corruption task force (a program established in addition to the British leadership of the national police and the British Accountant General who had found that one-quarter of government salaries went to dead or nonexistent employees, and who struggled to institute some measure of legality in the national finances), spoke of his "moment of madness" in taking this assignment.

"I'm an optimist by nature," Russell said, and his crisp khakis and neatly clipped silver hair, his quick smile and dark eyes that seemed to hold flecks of tinsel, matched his self-description. He looked and sounded like a man who generally thought himself lucky. But the culture of corruption here was "a mountain, four thousand meters high, requiring picks and carabiners and crampons," and he doubted that he and the Sierra Leoneans he was trying to train could surmount it. We talked on the dingy, quavering plane of a local airline willing to fly from Guinea into Sierra Leone, talked of the graft that permeated every level of government, from "the lowest functionary wanting his five hundred leones," his twenty-five cents, to the eight separate departments of inspectors awaiting their payoffs with every container that came in at the docks, to the ministers whose extortion went unchecked by the president, who was either too frightened to rein in his cabinet or making a discreet fortune for himself. But in one place, the national airport, Russell said, smiling and focusing on the positive, his task force had gotten bribery under control.

We landed with a clatter and a leaking of thick, scarlet palm oil from the baggage rack overhead, then walked through the desolate terminal, getting our passports stamped by a man behind one rickety table and our bags waved through, unchecked, by a man at another. As we waited for the helicopter that would take us on into Freetown, a passenger from our plane, a Lebanese, came along, as did one of the Sierra Leoneans from the immigration tables, a Buddha-like figure despite his aviator shades. With no concern for who might be watching, the Lebanese stuffed a wad of cash into the Buddha's breast pocket. "Well, as I said, we do have a bit of work to do," Russell laughed.

Ian Stuart smiled and laughed less often. With twenty years experience in the third world, he was here to oversee Britain's programs and advisors, from governance to infrastructure to agrisystems, for its Department for International Development. Looking fifteen or twenty-five years into the future, he didn't see much chance for the country's prosperity. "With peace and good governance, Sierra Leone might be able to quit importing rice. It might be able to feed itself." That was about the best that could be hoped for. Agriculture, he predicted, would never develop to profitability, because traditional land use—systems of land tenure that left plots small and rights uncertain—could not sustain mechanization. "So you're left with the primitive farming you see now: by hand, people stooped over with little hoes." I had seen it—and hadn't seen even a single animal-drawn plow in all my travels through Sierra Leone.

Tourism, Stuart projected, might bring some revenue, assuming Europeans ever returned to the beaches. And rutile, a mineral exported for the manufacture of paint, would help, if mining started back up. As for diamonds, they could make a degree of difference, if managed rather than smuggled. (The British planned to put an advisor on the diamond industry right at Kabbah's side, as an unofficial minister. But this was no guarantee that the president would be able or willing to clean up all the illicit exporting, even if his government were to control all the mines. Though foreign aid supplied about 70 percent of the nation's budget, and though much of that aid might well evaporate if the British gave up on the country and gave the sense that its situation was hopeless, still there were limits to the changes the British could muscle into reality. Nor had the diamond trade, always hard to regulate, been terribly clean a half century ago, when the English had been in full rule.) But tourism, in Stuart's eyes, was a dream with modest potential. Once, vacationers had supported a few hotels, but they'd never come in great numbers. And for all the media's easy talk of Sierra Leone as "resource-rich," the nation's minerals would probably never be enough. As I listened, it seemed that the respite in the war, the removal of immediate blight, had made the country's dismal prospects acutely clear. This was a place the world had long ago passed by. And with factors like a literacy rate of less than 30 percent, it was going to be generations before the country could catch up, even slightly. If it ever could. The future he saw seemed to leave Sierra Leone as close to the stone age as to the modern world.

"When we go," Major Jonathan Borthwick said in May 2001, thinking far ahead to the end of his country's engagement, "it will be like taking your hand out of a bucket of water."

In stints that usually lasted several months, the British soldiers cycled in and out—and always they arrived with high ambitions. Borthwick had come in March. Partly to oversee the new S.L.A.'s forward positions, partly to give advanced training, he was stationed in a tiny camp at the northern edge of the cease-fire lines, close enough to the rebel's uncertain intentions that, if you awoke with dysentery in the hushed darkness, you had to recall code words, passed around each evening at dusk, in order to make your way in one piece to the latrine.

To drop me at the camp, Foday had driven me beyond dozens of roadblocks: new S.L.A. troops requesting a "morale boostah" (that is, the price of a plastic baggie of liquor sold at the roadside stands); Civil Defense Forces gunmen half-demanding and half-begging for cigarettes; and little children with their own scraps of string held across the road. The six-year-olds wanted something, anything, to make them like the soldiers they imitated. Naked but for rag shorts, their lengths of string seemed about all they had. We couldn't drive through them, for pity and, too, for fear of older, armed siblings who might be watching from the jungle, ready to take revenge. But we were angry at all the stopping, and at the brazenness of these runtish boys. "No. We have nothing," I said through the window, and a kid pointed at a few tissues lying on the dashboard. Foday handed them out, four dusty tissues in all. The children danced.

We reached a U.N. checkpoint, past a settlement of U.N. tents surrounded by a mud village of quasi-prostitutes who served the peacekeepers as local wives. (The U.N. was gradually increasing its force in the country to 17,000.) The checkpoint was the U.N.'s last. A sergeant studied my press card, and wrote my name on a scrap from a Rice Krispies box. From then on, the route was thoroughly deserted. "Praise God, nothing will happen to me," Foday prayed, and talked of ambushes, and delivered a parable on the rebels' sincerity about peace: "You know dog? You know puppy? Puppy, you give new name. But dog? Craze dog? You getting me clear?"

The forest devouring the road was in fact less ominous these days—even as thousands of armed teenagers roamed the country in scant communication with the leaders who'd signed the cease-fire—and my early mornings in the British outpost could seem purged of everything except hope. In the hour before dawn, drums and singing wakened the world. The music came from the edge of the camp, where the government soldiers stayed, or just beyond. Hearing it—that fast rhythm, that slow high-pitched voice singing words I couldn't understand—I reminded myself of the night's code and slipped away from my cot in the thatch lean-to, searching for the music's source. Dawn didn't come gradually there but all at once; before, I needed my flashlight to navigate past the rotting army truck, the trees split by lightning and others by shrapnel, and across the plateau of scrub toward the dark sheds where I thought the singer might be. I wanted to listen up close to his elongated notes, stretching above the tight drumbeats. I wanted to see his face in the first light.

I turned off the main path toward the shed where my ears directed me. The music ceased. I stood in the middle of the field, waiting. The shed was still a good distance away, and I couldn't be sure the singer was there. Dawn neared. The Sierra Leonean soldiers would be stirring, and I felt a bit foolish, viewing myself as they might view me, a white man stumbling through the scrub, hunting for a morning song they took for granted.

I headed back toward the British lean-to. The music started again. I looked behind me, pinpointed another shed, followed the sound. It died, drifting notes dissipating in the humid air. I turned back once more, was beckoned yet again by the same melody from another, farther place. I told myself to try one last time, and one last time the notes faded to stillness, then to a rooster's strangulated cry, before I could reach them. Daylight had arrived.

And with it Major Borthwick taught an advanced class for platoon leaders. Even if the war came to a permanent end, the government was going to need, as much as anything, a dependable army behind it, a deterrent to the next R.U.F., or to the reincarnation of this one, so democracy would have time to spread roots. Ten Sierra Leonean captains and lieutenants sat on a fallen tree trunk, as Borthwick drew strips of colored ribbon from a little green cinch sack and gathered fallen mangoes from the ground. With these, on a patch of dirt, he laid out a map of reconnaissance paths and enemy positions and government platoons.

This was the way patrols and attacks were planned in the field, with rudimentary equipment like this, even in a first-world army. The British were teaching their own technique, and Borthwick, gray hair full and thick body packed with energy, danced over his map, adding a pile of stones to signify an enemy village. He began: "Even the best-trained troops in the world get lost."

He told a story of the Falklands, of British soldiers, veered astray, "cut up" by machine gunners from their own side. "Now, hands up, anyone who's ever been lost on patrol."

The students laughed. There was no shortage of hands. One belonged to Saidu Kamara, the science teacher I'd met long ago, the man who'd suffered the renegade soldiers raping neighborhood girls in his house, the man whose five-year-old brother had suffocated when the soldiers set Kamara's house ablaze. He had chosen to fight for his nation's sanity. Slightly built and soft-spoken as ever, his intelligence was hard to miss even behind his timidity, and he'd been promoted quickly by the British-led army. Leaning forward on the log, he felt a rapport with Borthwick. "He was quite candid with us," Kamara said later of the major, who gestured down at his map of mangoes with a retractable steel pointer, talked again of the "blue on blue clash" in the Falklands, and warned anyone who became a company commander to give the platoon leaders plenty of time to plan their front-line moves, "because remember, he is the poor sod whose ass is going out on the line . . . "

"Right, then," Borthwick said in crisp British transition. "Now none of the great panjandrums are here, so let's kick it around a bit." He closed up his pointer and opened the class up for questions, standing above the students but never talking down to them.

That evening we boiled ration packs with another major, one who'd come to the end of his tour. "I'm well aware," Major Bailey turned to me, after talking of wanting someday to open a jazz club in London, "that I'm speaking to someone who's going to write about this. But you might as well know the truth. There's no way to train these people in six months or three years or five. Maybe in three hundred. There's a lot we could learn from them. The kindness. But there's a force of nature at work. A sub-human intelligence. They're not a sub-race exactly, but . . . "

His voice drifted off in dejection. His tone wasn't that of invective but that of surrender. His height and muscle vanished as he sat hunched over, wilting into the foil pouch he ate from. And though I stiffened at his words, and though I would have chosen a logic that didn't deal in race, it was hard to ignore the pervasive inertia and seeming indifference he reacted to.

When I went to see Borthwick again two months later, he had been overwhelmed by the sense of impossibility and spoke in tones full of spite. "They've managed to *fuck* their own country," he railed, scraping carbon from rifles the Sierra Leonean troops had been given and failed to care for and returned inoperable to their saviors. He was supposed to be teaching specialty skills and guiding at brigade level. Instead, he chiseled black crust from clogged barrels. And meanwhile his partner went out to tighten the foresight screws of an entire battalion, because the soldiers weren't checking them and the aiming devices were falling to the forest floor. Hour after hour, his fatigues a body-glove of sweat, he hiked through the sprawling encampment of yet another company, little screwdriver in hand. "They can't do anything," Borthwick said, standing beside his truck with the emblem of the British mission, a white hand shaking a black one above the words "Trust and Teamwork," "without a white man standing over them."

As he got into the truck, the door, just fixed by a Sierra Leonean mechanic back at headquarters in Freetown, promptly fell off its hinges. It was the kind of slapstick that could have happened anywhere, but here it was symbolic. While a shortage of large military transport trucks had always been a problem for government defenders, three or four sat idle in the field behind Borthwick, greenery starting to consume them.

I heard it over and over, that this was a land of black adult children lost without the direction of a paternal white hand—and half-lost even as Father stood near. (I heard it not only from the British military. Some aid workers and rights advocates spoke a quiet, regretful, off-the-record version—"I never thought I'd hear myself saying this . . . "—as they acknowledged their think-

ing that a period of recolonization might be the only hope for
setting the country on a better path.) "They have the attention
span of a goldfish," a U.K. instructor said at the main base,
where troops, already graduated from basic training, showed up
for live-fire attack drills without their helmets, or forgot which
way to direct their guns, so that they aimed at their own army
rather than guarding against ambush, or, when told to stay low
as their squads paused between forward movements, laid their
guns down beside them, laid their heads on the earth, and fell
sound asleep. Watching this, it was difficult to argue when the instructors said, "Their retention is not good" or "They're lazy" or
"It's an immature country, an immature people" or "Whatever
gets done we do for them" or, as the S.L.A. commanders had no
clue as to their numbers of men or stocks of ammunition, and
as the men continued to treat their sights like irrelevant ap-
pendages, "What they fail to do isn't a matter of training—it's
akin to putting your clothes on backwards" or "This is taking
care of what few liberal attitudes I brought" or "As soon as we go,
it's all finished."

The day of the prison trouble, of the stampede away from downtown, I spent part of the afternoon with Keith Biddle. Near the
middle of Freetown, the prison's cement walls had been strafed
during past coups and invasions, its immense iron doors pitched
wide, inmates pouring forth; the fortress-like structure occupied a central place in the traumatized psyche of the capital.
That morning, guards had been overpowered behind the walls,
the chaos loud enough to be heard outside them. The sound was
a reminder; it belonged to the ghost of recent mayhem, rampant
amputations, 300 Freetown policemen killed within the month
of January 1999. So, on the main street that ran past the gates,
government sentries and U.N. troops had sprayed bullets at the
sky, desperate to keep the prisoners inside and imagined rebel

invaders at bay. By late afternoon, the reminder still loomed. The fatal rush away from downtown was over, but behind the iron doors sixty inmates clustered defiantly out of their cells, and if the British police chief didn't get them back in by nightfall (there was no separate department of corrections; Biddle supervised just about everything related to the nation's law enforcement), he ran the risk of more panicked firing and a city sparked beyond control.

He looked like a man comfortable with a degree of anarchy. He had a big birdish nose and hair winging in all directions. As he paced the matted carpet in his office, waiting for news from the Sierra Leonean negotiators he'd assigned, a rib of boxers showed beneath his blue police shirt that had come untucked and climbed damply above his waist. One blue pants leg had somehow gotten stuck around his knee, exposing a full length of shin. He was a tall, almost inexhaustible figure, who saw himself as "a butterfly man" for the crises he flew between. He seemed an ungainly butterfly, appeared more like a frenetic professor. In any case, his energy was running out. When I'd introduced myself a few days ago, and told him I planned to write about the effort to turn the country around, he'd let his long loose body collapse onto his office couch, and laughed, a sharp jab of chuckling at the naivete of my project and his own.

He'd talked, fatigue taking hold, of the policemen's unspeakably low pay, their unlivable barracks, their entrenched expectation of bribes, arrests being something the accuser paid for. He'd talked of the country in general: "These are good people, talented people; they only need education." His voice had passion, engagement, caring, yet it faded to a weary mumble. Today, having paced long enough, he bounded from his office down a lightless stairwell, in a building that looked halfway toward dereliction, to the room where his Sierra Leonean deputies might have an update. The inmates, he learned, were still out, and, worse, one of his top aides, whom Biddle had sent to collect riot kits—gas, clubs, masks—from another station, hadn't returned;

he'd gone off on a mission of his own devising. Biddle was left without a fallback of force, and darkness was an hour away.

"For fuck's sake," he snapped, "I told him gear for two hundred men and he done what appealed to him at the moment. They don't fucking do as they're told. The longevity of their thought is about this far. They just can't plan for what will happen."

Biddle's program was to delegate as much decision-making as possible, to build Sierra Leonean leadership, but now he drove to the prison. "I tell them to put men with riot kits, and instead I've got men with guns," which would be a liability inside the prison, where they might be wrestled away. "I tell them to surround the perimeter, and you can see how well that's been done." He pointed toward the few groups of sentries with assault rifles gathered here and there outside the walls, chatting amidst the jagged cement pillars of torched houses or staring with glazed eyes, no longer looking terrified so much as benumbed, the torpor of existing in a land of war having replaced the morning's panic.

But trouble, for that day, had started to float elsewhere. Some of the inmates had returned to their cells by the time Biddle assembled what riot squad he could muster, five or six in gasmasks, with no gas, to accompany him inside. He asked me to wait, then went to try to get the remaining holdouts back in, disappearing behind the iron doors.

A thousand men and boys, in underwear or old clothes worn thin as paper, dug into the bowels of the town. They pried with their shovels under the school, swung their picks into the floor of the bygone police station, burrowed under the stores and houses, searching for diamonds. Here there seemed to be no law whatsoever. When I ventured through one of the biggest pits, a ravine, thirty or so feet deep, that started under the abandoned school and snaked out into the jungle, diggers in packs of forty,

fifty, seventy surrounded me, pressing, shouting, alternately
threatening me with hoes and holding out "stones" in the palms
of their hands, urging me to buy.

This was Koidu, where the alluvial gravel held the country's
highest quality diamonds, and it was still, in September 2001,
controlled by the R.U.F. But control was a misleading concept.
On the main road stood a metal shipping container, with two little holes punched raggedly into the sides for air, that served as
the R.U.F.'s prison. And back at rebel headquarters in Makeni a
few months earlier, in a dusky office above a wary street, Gibril
Massaquoi, one of the two men who'd taken over for Sankoh
when the Papa was captured, had lectured me on the "civilian"
authorities the R.U.F. established in its territory, with "people's
courts" and "as you have seen, even a police for traffic movement." Yes, at the Makeni roundabout I had seen the teenager in
the uniform taken from a U.N. peacekeeper; I had seen him
staring at any driver who dared enter town. But by now, out in
Koidu, all order was disintegrating.

For the sake of calm, mining was supposed to be in morato-
rium during the peace process, but the U.N. troops, which had
by September deployed throughout the country, avoided the pits
as much as they could, glancing skittishly away when they drove
by, because, one captain explained, "The rebels don't like us
to look." The rebels, even in dissolution, still intimidated the
peacekeepers, but lately they hadn't been strong enough to keep
the Civil Defense Forces out of the town or away from the mining; they'd been forced to share a portion of power and gravel,
and now the two enemies dug in wild and sometimes explosive
proximity, separated only by a few feet of mud. It was a free for
all in the pits, an orgy of spades and sifters, an underworld of
diggers half-submerged in opaque water, a madness of long-
muscled undernourished arms shaking large wire saucers laden
with rocks and of hands caressing gravel, trying to coax to the
surface a tiny pebble that gleamed. The only thing clear was that
the government wouldn't be getting any revenue from this

earth. As I walked through the market, a dozen men hissed at me and licked their palms, an open signal that they had gems to sell and that I had only to swallow them in order to get them home. From here the diamonds would be carried through the jungle and sold over the border or dealt to traders with their own schemes. An Australian I met at Paddy's related his: He inspected and negotiated for a parcel of stones in Koidu, had rebel officers deliver a specially sealed box to Guinea, paid off government ministers to make sure his smugglers had no trouble, and arranged for a Guinean certificate of origin. He paid for no licenses or taxes, and, with the Guinean certificate, didn't have to worry about the international ban on the "blood diamonds" that were funding civil wars in the Democratic Republic of the Congo and Angola as well as here. The Australian's gems could move easily on to cutters and polishers, to Western jewelers and stores.

So with collusion and disregard all the way up the line, the trade thrived. Did any of the profit stay in the half-deserted, deeply excavated town? There was no sign of it, besides a few beer halls. The top rebel and Civil Defense Forces leaders must have been exerting exactly enough order to enrich themselves amidst the disarray, or to bolster hidden stockpiles of weapons. There must have been that level of law at work while the diggers hacked through the floors, while men sold off the corrugated roofs, while trees and elephant grass erupted inside the remaining shells as though within walled gardens. "Look at the richest place in Sierra Leone," a boy told me, pointing around us in disgust. The town had been devoured.

"This is the carcass of a state," Corinne Dufka said, on her way to collect evidence for Human Rights Watch. "The law doesn't function in Sierra Leone, even within the government-controlled areas. The British are making a real effort, and there are courageous and good police officers who are trying. But this is a lawless society. It's a moral garbage dump. And without the rule

of law, without a judicial system that works, all the efforts to rescue Sierra Leone are going to be like trying to put Humpty
Dumpty back together again."

Corinne had been everywhere, seen everything, but she'd
never been anywhere like this. She'd left California to do social
work amidst El Salvador's civil war in the '80s, sometimes taking
photographs so the families of the missing "could look through
my very macabre photo album and perhaps be able to identify
their loved ones." Then a close friend, the man who'd first
taught her to work in a darkroom, was shot and killed during the
country's violent elections. Another Reuters photographer was
wounded there, a bullet through the lung; the agency needed
someone to take their places; Corinne volunteered.

"Didn't that give you any pause?" I asked, as we climbed up
into the peninsular hills, the pillowy jungle banks decorated with
ribbons of white smoke from the cooking fires of hidden settlements. "Two friends shot within a month?"

"No," she said, "I didn't have any hesitation. That was happening all the time in El Salvador. If anything it just made me
more motivated." She talked of documenting abuses, of "communicating to people and raising their consciousness and in-
forming public policy"; she spoke in the language of Berkeley,
where her career in social work had begun. Then she added,
without apology, "And it was an opportunity for me as a professional." She wanted to be a war-zone photographer, and bullets,
appropriately, had cleared the way.

Tall and dark-haired, with girlish eyes and a way of walking
through the world that wasn't girlish at all—"She is one very
strong woman," Neall said, as though paying tribute to another
soldier—she went next to the Balkans, to the Bosnian-Croat
lines. Reuters provided an armored Land Rover to keep her safe
from crossfire; in it, she and two colleagues headed toward a
town in flames. "It was actually I who wanted to go," she remembered. "Because of the fires. And we drove down this street. And
a little voice inside me said, No, don't go down that street, be-

cause there's debris, there's tons of debris, and you should always be careful because it can hide land mines. But I didn't listen, and we made a collective decision to go down. I think part of it was that . . ." She stared away out her window, up at the smoke ribbons rising to join the mist at the crest of the hills. She seemed about to speculate on the things, immediate or far in the past, that had led her along that route, and on the things that might have saved her, but behind her black blouse and floral skirt, somewhere near the core of her slender body, she was exactly what Neall could see: a soldier. "Anyway," she cut herself off, "it was a mistake. We made an error of judgment.

"So we went about twenty meters down. And all I remember was a huge—a huge ball of the brightest orange, like the center of the sun, and I remember thinking, We *really* shouldn't have gone down this street. And then: the doors were blown out, and I was kind of half in and half out, and all I knew was that there was blood everywhere. But I didn't realize where it was from. I was completely out of it. I guess my first thought was that the car was going to explode, so I just remember walking out into the middle of all this burning, and it was misty, a thick-thick mist like that on the hills, and I touched myself. Okay, you've got our arms. Your legs are there. Blood *everywhere* and I couldn't figure out where it was coming from, and it was from here, this scar here." She touched the white seam that angled from lip to jaw.

"I'd had my camera near my lap, and with a land mine the force comes straight upward. My camera cut completely through my face. I walked about ten meters. I had this cashmere scarf I'd just bought in London, and I loved that scarf. It was so warm, and I put it there on my face. Then I just collapsed. The Croats on the hill were sniping, aiming down at us. I couldn't move from the middle of the street. I'd been wounded in both legs. My knees were wrecked. But the Croats were playing; they could have gotten me anyplace they wanted."

One of her colleagues managed to lift her over his shoulder and get her behind a wall. Legs shattered and pinned in the mangled car, it was all her other colleague could do to drag himself onto the pavement. He lay beside two more mines, until the Bosnians, who'd set them, slid out through the sniper fire to carry the journalists to a nearby garage. Legs were set with splints of cardboard boxes. Turkish coffee was served in little white porcelain cups. The U.N. evacuated the wounded to a British field hospital. "Do you think I'll need stitches?" Corinne asked a nurse.

"Can I get you a mirror?" the nurse answered.

"No, thank you."

The nurse brought one anyway. Corinne could see her teeth without opening her mouth. Her face, from her lower lip downward, hung open like a flap.

"And then I realized," she laughed, as we lurched and bumped down out of the hills toward a refugee camp, "that my modeling career was over."

Months after leaving Bosnia in '93, she was crouched in Somalia, half-healed and unable to run from the Mogadishu streets that burst into battle around her; then, winning awards, she was sent to southern Sudan and Liberia, Ethiopia and the D.R.C., Burundi and Rwanda. In Rwanda she captured the faces of corralled Tutsis waiting for extermination; in Liberia she got close enough to a street execution to photograph the bullet flying from the barrel. For ten years she got close enough to go numb. In '98, covering the Congolese civil war when the U.S. embassy in Nairobi was bombed, what she thought, seeing the images of hundreds of maimed Kenyans on CNN, was that the pictures in the newspapers wouldn't be hers. "I was crying my eyes out, and I was far more upset about having missed the opportunity as a photojournalist than I was about what had happened." She had traveled a long way from "communicating to people and raising their consciousness." Crying in front of CNN in a Congolese hotel room, she told herself, "Get the fuck out of this profession."

From above, as we came out of the hills, the refugee camp was an orderly layout of white tents, a suburban town of canvas set on a perfect grid. Then, as we neared, the white took on its glaze of mud, and once we parked, the grid became a maze of dormant life and flourishing disease, of children, naked from the waist down, sweating in strange milky beads. Clipboard under her arm, Corinne asked along the alleys for the witness she'd come to find, an old man who, she'd heard, had survived a mass slaughter, dozens locked in a large hut, flame put to thatch. Human Rights Watch had sent her here two years ago to take testimonials from men like Lamin, testimonials that filled long press releases and reports whose plea to the Western world could be summarized in three words: Make this stop. But lately her mission had broadened. There was talk of a tribunal, stirrings of an international court, sponsored by the U.N., coming to Sierra Leone. The U.N. had attached a last-second, little-noticed rider to the amnesty granted in '99, an allowance that crimes against humanity could be prosecuted. For those who'd ordered the war's atrocities, justice would at last arrive. And unlike the tribunals for the Balkans and Rwanda, this one would be held in the country itself and headed by a mixture of expatriate and local judges. Justice would happen at home, and Corinne saw the special court as a chance to implant the idea of the rule of law in "a society where law is meaningless." If the court ever convened, she wanted to be sure the worst offenders came before it, and she didn't want any of them walking away with acquittals. She wanted people to see—and internalize—what the law could do. So with her translator, Saphi, who wore a long blue-and-white church dress and pointy high-heeled shoes, she searched out witnesses from border to border, ducking now into one of the broiling tents, where a withered man sat motionless on a splintered bench, sat alone as though he'd been waiting there for days or weeks or months for the chance to tell his story.

"The special court can break the bubble of impunity," Corinne believed, thinking not only of the war's terror but of a level of brutality that had come to seem almost acceptable throughout the society. She'd talked of a case in an upcountry town, a girl raped and made pregnant by her fifty-four-year-old teacher, who simply offered the family a monthly stipend to keep them from pressing charges. With such an income at stake, the family wanted no part of the police. And even if they had wished for punishment more than money, and even if the police would take action without payment, the provinces had no courts to try major crimes; pressing charges would have meant a journey to Freetown, many hours away, then living there in a state of indefinite suspension, waiting for years for a trial that might never begin.

I asked Corinne if a situation like this was less an emblem of a legal vacuum than a vestige of indigenous law, compensation being a traditional remedy even for violent crime.

"It's the worst of both worlds," she said, and spoke of the war's corrupting effect on the local chiefs who oversaw the customary courts, the near absence of residual societal structures, traditional or modern. (Abdul Tejan-Cole, the Sierra Leonean lawyer and human rights activist, had told me much the same thing, except that he traced the breakdown of customary systems back thirty years, to when the national dictator of the time had begun appointing chiefs to consolidate his own power, rather than letting the chiefs be selected by long-honored means.) "People become very fatalistic," Corinne went on. "There's not the will or the expectation of justice. The poor feel that justice is beyond their reach. Full stop. Just beyond their reach. 'We na de poor man, de poor man no get justice.' All of the institutions that are supposed to be upholding the rule of law have been key protagonists in the problem. How can you have the police, who are some of the prime violators of the rule of law, upholding the rule of law? Justice is bought. Justice is a privilege. So the very concept of justice goes missing from Sierra Leone society."

Her dream for a special court was like a vision of mass awakening, brought by the Western judges who, she expected, would lead the tribunal. As perpetrators on all sides were held accountable, people would witness the law's power. "This is an opportunity for the international community to impose the value of justice. And it's okay to impose values on a society that's so completely fucked up."

Corinne sat next to the old man, close to the old man. She touched him on his macheted wrist. At furious speed, she wrote down everything he said, filling the pages on her clipboard with red ink.

Yet sometimes she felt a despondence that crossed a border into disgust. When she talked of the nation as "a moral garbage dump" she meant not only its institutions and most obvious criminals; she felt a void of conscience everywhere. "Everybody's angling for advantage. There are no friendships. There is no trust. Everyone's playing for a weakness. Everyone's stealing. It's what's expected. The terms of human interaction."

She understood all too well that extreme poverty and extreme warfare had been causes of what she perceived, "that these people have been beaten down until they have absolutely no other alternative," and she understood that the color of her skin—and the wealth that whiteness presumably brought—reduced her to an objectified figure of rescue. Sierra Leoneans in general didn't beg openly. There were few hands or cups held out on the streets. But they besieged her with a kind of friendship that turned quickly to scams, to funds needed for invented emergencies—funds that went for the perpetual emergency of daily living—so that the line every white heard relentlessly, "I would like to be your friend," had come to mean only one thing, "I would like to have some of your money."

She recognized that being white skewed what she saw of the people she lived among, cut her off from their better selves, "but I start to lose faith," she said, faith that those better selves existed. She lived close to Lamin's amputee camp and knew many of its victims, and I'd heard her rail—as I'd heard relief workers rail—about their conniving, about their embrace of indigence for the sake of soliciting money, about their overtures of friendship. She talked of Somalia as the ultimate lost state, a nation without any government at all, but of Sierra Leone as the ultimate land of lost people, where basic morality, basic sentiment, basic pride seemed so often at a premium.

"I hate it," she said of the times when she sank into feeling this way. She rebuked herself for lost empathy, realized that she could never take into sufficient account the way people here had suffered. Not religious in the least, she thought of visiting an Italian priest in Freetown for counsel. But her religion was the notion of justice. To avenge the suffering would help restore the society. It was as though she saw the special court as a kind of superego. Run fairly and effectively, it would not only show what the rule of law could accomplish, it would work at levels less conscious: to strengthen the attenuated sense of right and wrong, an attenuation, in the highest perpetrators and the most abject victims, that seemed to narrow everyone's humanity.

The old man had on a white dress shirt deteriorated to gauze, a red-and-blue plaid fishing cap with colorless homemade fringe around the crown. Just above the wrists, his forearms took a twenty-five degree turn. The amputation squad had failed to cut completely through; the wounds had healed at this angle; his hands lay useless in his lap, fingers unable to close and thumbs capable only of slight pressure. Sitting across from him on a low stool, maybe two feet away and at eye-level with his maiming, my eyes glazed and eyelids sagged; my neck snapped as Corinne started to take his testimony. If Saphi hadn't touched my shoulder I might have nodded off. It's possible to say that I was overwhelmed by his wounds, his experience, that sometimes it was all too much, and that sleep was my escape. This would be partly true. But partly, too, I had been immersed in so much horror that I wasn't powerfully moved. Here was another man crippled, another story that would have seemed, when I'd first read of this war, impossibly cruel. It was half-normal now, its drama not enough to counter the heat.

Corinne was tireless. She asked questions and filled sheets so fast that Saphi had to remind her, "Corinne, are you paging?"

The old man, a farmer from the east, had once had two wives, seven children. The family had scattered when the rebels attacked their village. But the man, with three of his grown daughters, had been caught, herded and locked into a hut.

"Locked?" Corinne prodded for inconsistency. "Could the mud hut be locked?"

The door had been wood. It had been padlocked. But not before the man was yanked outside. " 'Pa,' " he remembered them saying, " 'we going to cut your hands.' " He asked to be killed instead. "But they say whatever has been decided is what must happen."

Then, wrists dangling and rebels smoking marijuana, he watched the hut become a crematorium with his daughters inside.

Had any of the captives tried to force their way out?

At first, yes, before the door was locked. One or two had charged free, somehow escaped the rebels' guns. But after the door was shut again, and a small padlock put on, everyone had submitted.

Repeatedly Corinne asked if he knew the names of any of the rebels that day. He recalled hearing one, but not one belonging to any of the leaders. She pressed for identifying details. "When those people get hold of you," he explained, "you lose your sense."

For the purpose of the special court, this wasn't going to be a fruitful interview, but she continued on, eliciting the old man's journey to the nearest hospital outside rebel territory, the way he'd walked for two days, cradling his hands in front of him, bracing them against his forearms. Scratchy and strained, his voice matched his age. Emotion didn't pour through. Most of the time, it was hard to tell whether there was much emotion left. But when Corinne asked whether the people inside the burning hut had made any sound, the tent we sat in might have been on fire. "Heeewh! Heeeewh! Heeeeewh!" he cried, mimicking their syllable, voice raspy and high and full of surprise, as though in the final moments, no one, no matter how much they'd seen and heard in their country, could believe this was really happening.

Chanting soon replaced the old man's cry—chanting and drumming from outside the tent. And when Corinne finished the interview, and we walked to the camp's edge, we had another lesson in why the rule of law might be a long way off.

Next to the camp, a roadside store had been robbed. The night before, thieves had hacked through the mud wall, making off, the owner claimed, with $1,500 worth of goods. It was hard to believe that the mud box could hold that value in cigarettes and beer, razor blades and batteries, but everyone agreed—the squat woman who was the owner and the drummer who accompanied the bush devils and the crowd from the camp—that the owner would pay the bush devils $350 if they revealed the criminals.

One of the bush devils, the figures half-belonging to the underworld who had the power to catch and nullify evil, wore a red robe that appeared to have gathered all the soil and filth of a subterranean existence, and, on his head, a black wooden box with black horns ensnared in a random web of wires and rags and mosquito netting. His partner's headdress, an eruption of thick roots, crowned the costume of a court jester: red baggy pants and yellow socks with no shoes. Their faces were covered in black cloth.

An hour ago, the owner had hidden "a small something"— she wouldn't disclose what—somewhere nearby, around the store or in the camp. If the bush devils proved their power by finding it, she would pay them the first half of the $350. When they caught the thieves (who, everyone felt, came from the camp or the adjacent village), she would pay the final installment. What would follow this conviction was unclear, probably a beating and flogging.

A police station stood less than a mile down the road. There, in the main room that felt like a dungeon, the senior officer said that though the robbery hadn't yet been reported, it soon would be. "They come like rain here," he spoke softly, of the victims seeking justice. He had one partner; otherwise the place was completely empty. "They come by the thousands." A wiry middle-aged man lost in a large hand-me-down blue uniform, he talked of upholding "the laws of England" and of the hunting societies kidnapping local children, even children from the nearby police barracks, seizing them for indoctrination or—and the sense I had was of something occasional—sacrifice. He may have invented the thousands who sought out the police, but he didn't seem to have lost his mind. Yet I could never hear this sort of thing—whether from Foday or from a chemistry teacher who spoke of juju men and the blood of virgins—without wondering if the speaker had. The police station was barely an hour's drive outside the capital.

Back by the store, the bush devils' entourage drummed on red wooden boxes and plucked at an instrument with three metal keys, prongs nailed to a board. A bush devil's aide, red and yellow yarn cascading from his head, hurled a raw egg at the store's back wall. The bush devils circled through the camp, not dancing, not peering, not searching in any apparent way, just walking, as if aimlessly. Following them, a man bore a tortoise shell bowl filled with special brown water. Women and children kept a cautious distance, but here, unlike Foria, they were allowed to watch. The yellow socks wandered again toward the store. Saphi, daughter of a paramount chief with twelve wives and more concubines, convert to an evangelical Christianity, had fled to Foday's car. In her church dress and high heels, she sat in the front seat, clutching the Bible she always kept with her. "I counsel, I destroy, I uproot, I cast away, I take absolute control," she repeated over and over, and tried to convince herself: "God will send the Holy Ghost fire to destroy them. It will consume

them." The faceless men beneath those horns and roots were
"full of evil spirits," she took a few seconds to tell me, before returning to her frantic prayers.

The aide flung another egg. The bush devils studied the pattern of its splatter. The red and yellow yarn rushed toward a
shanty beside the store. The drumming intensified. A man dug
with his fingers at the base of a pole. He held up a fifty leone
coin. Now the process of catching the thieves—ritual hours, ritual days—could begin. The owner confirmed it: The devils had
found what she had hidden, a single coin that could have been
anywhere within acres.

Laying aside her Bible when we had driven safely away, Saphi
talked of what beings with occult powers, like the bush devils,
could do. "When the witch wants to make it," she said, "he will
give you meningitis." She laughed almost bitterly at Corinne's
skepticism, and told her, "We have grown up and seen things you
have not seen. We have grown up and seen people sorcering.
This is Africa." Foday laughed with her, at our ignorance. They
knew the possibility of evil all around them. "The whites"—Saphi
rubbed the skin of her forearm in a gesture not of self-hatred
but of superiority—"they want to believe only what they see with
their own eyes."

TWELVE

Why do you stay here?
Mary and Paul Kortenhoven had two grand-
children of Foria. Peter had been born to their son Matthew and
his girlfriend Kumba; Lydia, to their daughter, Sarah, and her
boyfriend Fasalie, a young farmer soon to be a leader in the Civil
Defense Forces. And certainly the grandchildren, though born
several years before the war and gone before it began, were part
of why Mary and Paul had remained so long in Sierra Leone,
why they had remained through everything. Certainly Peter and
Lydia were part of the unbreachable connection their grandpar-
ents felt with the country, a bond that sometimes filled me with
awe but that could stir as well self-reproach and undercurrents
of aversion—whenever my own emotional failings, my need for
disengagement, took hold—so that sometimes I had to stop myself from asking, Why do you stay here? for fear that an edge of
harsh incredulity and even distaste would transform my question
into, How can you possibly stay here? or, Why don't you just go
home? as if the failing were theirs and not my own.

There is a limit to what I can tell you of Peter and Lydia, who
were sixteen and thirteen when I met them. I didn't ask them to
agree to a reporter's prying, to having the details of their lives
made public. It didn't seem necessary. I will say only that, for
Mary and Paul, seeing their children immersed in the Kuronko
community (where Sarah's best friend, Duko, had been married
off at around the age of fourteen to a chief with almost twenty
wives) to the point of having babies when Matthew was eighteen
and Sarah, seventeen, was not the kind of immersion they'd
wished for when they'd begun their mission. "Did I ever think,
What did we do? Why did we ever come to Sierra Leone?" Paul
laughed, remembering. "Did I ever think about beating the crap

out of Fasalie? Well, I probably *should* have beaten the crap out
of him. But I didn't." And undoubtedly, though children born
out of wedlock were not in the least unusual among the Kuranko, it was terribly difficult for Kumba and Kumba's family
when her relationship with Matthew (he'd gone so far as to build
them a house in Foria and to clear her a farm) fell apart: when
their plans for marriage evaporated as he went back to the States
for college; as he fell in love; as he married. Until Kumba's father drifted off to another village with a second wife, he had
been adamant in demanding money from the Kortenhovens, a
bride-price though there had been no wedding. The Kortenhovens had promised to take care of Kumba instead, to support
her financially.

Until he was six, Peter was raised in Foria by Kumba and
Mary and Paul, then across the ocean by Peter's father and step-
mother. Lydia, meanwhile, had been toddling nearby when
Sarah, harvesting groundnuts, had sliced through that puff
adder. Nothing if not strong-willed, Sarah had never had any serious thought of marriage; without protest from Fasalie, she'd
taken Lydia with her when she moved back to America.

Given the possibilities, everything seemed to have worked
out well enough in the end, for the kids, for the families. From
Kumba, who had wound up marrying Joseph Sesay and settling
in Kabala, I never sensed any hint of lingering anger toward
Mary and Paul, and though it was possible to believe that this was
because the Kortenhovens still supplied her with bits of clothing
and cash, and because her husband was employed by the mission, it was also possible to feel a tranquility and tacit bond
between them. In any case, Mary still spoke of her as "my daughter." And for Mary and Paul, who'd struggled, at the time of the
pregnancies, to console themselves with the hope that "God was
still in control of the whole shebang," the end was "two beautiful, beautiful grandchildren."

Still, those grandchildren explained only a fraction of the
attachment between the Kortenhovens and Sierra Leone, and

as for why Mary and Paul had remained for two decades, the
existence of the grandchildren amplified as much as answered
the question. They amplified it because Peter and Lydia, with
Matthew and Sarah, lived where life was infinitely easier, in the
States.

On the drive northeast the mud booths of the R.U.F. roadblocks
had signs reading, "To All Motherfukkers" and "Merciful Killer."
We didn't have much trouble getting through, no one told to
"come down," to get out of the car. There were no payments
made, nothing more than brief discussions through open windows. It was the locals, loaded ten to a dragging sedan with
200,000 cratered miles of history in its chassis, who were
stopped, surrounded, made to pay. We, the whites in the Kortenhovens' S.U.V., were waved on. The cease-fire seemed to have restored that racial hierarchy to the rebel-held areas. The days of
killing or kidnapping missionaries and relief workers appeared
over.

A bit of everyday life had returned to the remote north as
well. People had come back to the decimated roadside villages,
and rice was spread on the pavement to dry. The few cars veered
around these half-moons of pale yellow; the road was meant far
more for fixing meals than for driving, here.

A pack of monkeys ran across. The bush closed in from both
sides. A taxi was unloaded—the tower of satchels deconstructed
from its roof—so that it might crawl uphill with the passengers
hauling their belongings behind it. This was how hills were
mounted. At the crest, the tower of sacks and jerricans and ancient suitcases would be rebuilt, and everyone could ride again,
including the boys with their feet planted wide on the slopes of
the rooftop pile, surfing the forest as the taxi hit fifty, plunging
down.

Kabala was nestled by hills. Here the Kortenhovens had fled
from Foria years ago; here the government held an island of

territory, surrounded by rebel terrain; here the Kortenhovens were starting their next project, a kind of vocational school for women like Koma Mansaray, who'd had a permanent "RUF" written with a broken soda bottle across her breasts.

Even with the cease-fire, the town of Kabala was as close to Foria as the Kortenhovens could safely work. Foria was just too cut off to be sure of anything. But the Kortenhovens wanted, at least, to visit the village they hadn't seen in four years, the village they still considered their African home. So we set out along the thirty miles of dirt track, which, because it was dry season, was merely slow, navigated at eight or ten miles per hour, with no spades or winches required.

Mary met her first old acquaintance halfway there. We had just passed the skeleton of a Nigerian truck, abandoned at the base of a hill, unable to climb with the fleeing soldiers it held. The troops had dived out and sprinted from the rebels; the truck was left to rot until only metal remained; and quickly the steel had been swallowed by jungle. From the jungle now a one-armed woman leapt in front of the S.U.V. We hadn't seen her approach; the forest was much too thick for that. One moment we were utterly alone; the next our way was blocked by an old amputee with bare flat breasts dangling to her belly.

Mary recognized her right away. It was Feremusu. She was not a war victim but an epileptic whose seizures had pitched her repeatedly into cooking fires, burning her arm enough times that the limb had grown fully necrotic, flesh dead to everything except disease, and had to be removed. She danced at Mary's open window, hopping with joy, singing in a raspy voice, "Mary, Mary, Mary, Mary, Mary." With equal joy, Mary laughed, blue-green eyes losing their pallor, their suggestion of gray. The two women clasped hands, saying almost nothing, the villager continuing her dance, sort of running in place and fitting her song, "Mary, Mary," to the rhythm of her steps. Then, as abruptly as she'd appeared, she vanished, bending almost double and darting back into the trees, invisible immediately, a withered, one-armed sprite who'd signaled the happiness of Mary's home-coming.

In Foria, the rebel reception was formal. A man wearing a white head rag, narrow shades, and a large bowie knife on his belt introduced himself as a lieutenant and led us to a central tree, to a wooden bench. Major Pack 'Em There, his name in Krio meaning "Pile 'Em Up," a reference to his many kills, welcomed us from the throne of his baby blue plastic lawn chair. After four attacks, four burnings, four flights and returns and rebuildings, the rebels and the villagers had reached a kind of equilibrium, the villagers feeding the rebels and suffering a relative minimum of harm: They were left alive, their limbs intact, though they played the games their guests requested, like "Chinese Thinking," in which a man was forced to cross his arms and grab his ears and then, on his elbows and toes, to arch himself belly-downward over a fire. And the community hadn't completely held together: Some had been like Duko, who had run off with a rebel commander, by choice, people later said.

Now, slouched with a silent transistor radio in one hand and a cigar-sized reefer in the other, the major stressed his adherence to peace: "When we say war done done, war done done!" A nine-year-old boy, AK-47 like a hugely oversized toy in his arms, stood guard behind him, eyeing us unreadably.

"We are not rebel, we are government!" the lieutenant announced his anticipation that a new power-sharing arrangement would be made.

"For a major, I know how much rice I get!" Pack 'Em There spoke vehemently of the in-kind pay he expected to receive when he was taken into the government army. (And throughout the country, pay was essential to surrender. For turning in their weapons, adult soldiers from all sides—R.U.F., West Side Boys, old army mutineers, hunting society militias—were promised a World Bank–funded "reintegration allowance" of $150, to tide them over between the life of looting and some blurry goal of employment.) Heatedly, distrustfully, Pack 'Em There went on about his future rice rations, as if we were here to decide them. But he and his henchmen appeared exhausted and sick as well as stoned—the whites of one captain's eyes were a lurid yellow— and eventually the vehemence subsided. "You are welcome," Pack 'Em There offered listlessly, slumping farther in his baby blue chair, assault rifle strewn on the ground at his feet. "You are welcome one hundred percent." The Kortenhovens were free to wander the village, to talk with the people of their home.

Paul, his health uncertain, his thyroid deteriorating and his heart soon to require an emergency flight to Europe for treatment, hadn't made the trip north, but Mary and Aaron—who had just finished college in the States and was living again in Sierra Leone—began walking separate routes through Foria, each trailed by an entourage of tugging children. The kids, too young to recall the Kortenhovens living here, felt their importance. (Their entourages were far bigger than the one attached to me, the unknown white visitor.) And when Mary stopped before the hut of someone she knew, there came inevitably, from the villager, a cry of pleasure, a smile of pleasure from Mary. Then followed an exchange of ritual greetings:

"*Tana-ma-tele?*"
"*Tana-wo-sa.*"
"*Ille dungh?*"
"*Allah tanto.*"

And next, after eight or ten of these scripted questions and replies, there was silence, a silence that began to seem monumental, merging as it did with the hush of extreme heat and surrounding jungle, a deadness of sound that felt overwhelming, despite the faint giggles of the crowding children. In this quiet, Mary moved on.

She wore a loose white T-shirt, loose pale khakis, took slow strides along the paths to another home, and another. The screams of joy; the ritual hellos; the end of speech. It didn't seem the reticence was being imposed by the rebels, who didn't follow her. It felt like something more. Her face seemed to pinch, her blue-green irises to drain of color, regaining a wash of gray. She was in her fifties, but started to walk at a pace that belonged to a woman much older. She came to the veranda of a blind man, performed the same pattern of conversation, gazed for a moment into his gorgeous, gem-like, blue, blank eyes. The silence had a palpable, crushing weight. Did she really have any meaningful connection at all with the people here? All of her years in Sierra Leone, in Foria, seemed to have left no deeper a link than this with a blind man who could not see her and to whom she had nothing to say. For hours she wound through the village, steps determined, dogged, scarcely quicker than sluggish yet not flagging, hut to hut, hut to hut, as though she had lived with the weight for decades. A man on a porch cut her slices of pineapple, painfully sweet. She ate in silence.

"Not friends," she would say to me that night in Kabala. "Not in the way you would use that word. There is no one here that I confide in. Not when we lived in Foria, either. I didn't become close with anyone in that way. What connects us is something different. It's all the things we've been through together. The measles epidemic. The cholera. The war. It's history, shared history."

More than twenty years ago, I thought, she had arrived in Sierra Leone. More than twenty years had passed by in a vacuum of friendship, a communion of plagues.

An acute sense of her solitude made it difficult for me to breathe. To give is to receive, I reminded myself.

But a life of giving could be lonelier than any on earth.

Yet driving back toward Kabala from Foria, Aaron, who was at the wheel, stopped the car suddenly. He, too, could seem a figure of striking isolation, his features sharp, as though keeping people at a careful distance came naturally. His shaggy blond hair and beard softened his face, but only so much, without affecting the privacy of his eyes. While Mary had hiked through the village, he had talked easily with the people in Foria—even without a hunting rifle or machete, a Kuronko cap on his head and kola nut in his mouth and cheap plastic sandals on his feet, even in khaki shorts and sturdy hiking boots, he was still the Kuronko white man—but I hadn't seen his long arms open to wrap around anyone, to recapture briefly, or just to recognize, the intimacy of old companionship.

When he stopped the car with Foria five or six miles behind us, I thought one of the tires had gone flat or that he was simply going to pee. He gave a sound that resembled his way of laughing, almost staccato. A second or two passed before I realized that he was crying. He opened his door just as Joseph Sesay, who'd been with the mission since Aaron was eight, and who'd ridden his Honda to Foria along with us, pulled up behind. Aaron reeled out of the car as Joseph walked up alongside. Their shoulders collided, and, looping his arms around Joseph's neck, tall body nearly collapsing, Aaron sobbed. Hugging, the two men lurched along the track, unsteady as drunkards, and turned, disappearing into the forest. Aaron's grief rose audibly from behind the vines and trees.

That night, under Kabala's star-blanched sky, I asked what had upset him. For the past half hour, he had been speaking angrily of the deprivation people faced, especially in the north, where Kabbah took no interest whatsoever. But it was clear that his sobbing had overtaken him from a deeper place, a more profound connection, than even his impassioned talk of village hardship could explain, and when I asked what had brought it on, he didn't hesitate. "More than you can say," he answered, and left it at that.

Koma Mansaray, one of the first students at the Kortenhovens' new women's center in Kabala, had spent the past two years walking the country with the rebels who had abducted her. She had begun her journey with a husband, a brother, and a year-and-a-half-old baby. Wanting use of her husband's taxi, and use of him as a driver, the soldiers had seized them all from her parents' Kabala home, burned the house, and, taking pity on the elders, left Koma's parents tied to a tree. When the car broke down, Koma's husband was forced from behind the wheel, pushed down on the road, his ears cut off, his hands cut off, his fading consciousness riddled with bullets until all life closed down. With that, the soldiers and their remaining captives started away on foot.

Now she was nineteen years old, she guessed. During a break between classes, with her hair woven in elaborate braids and sculpted in ribbon-like curls, and wearing a T-shirt, arrived from somewhere in another world, that proclaimed, "If You Don't Practice . . . You Don't Deserve to Dream," she said, "I don't talk nothing because me somebody afraid," giving the reason for her silence, her stillness, as her husband was sliced and shot. "I pray to God for me life."

There had been nothing she could do then; nothing she could do farther along on her journey, when, with her baby, Dura, tied to her back, she was ordered to drag corpses from Kono villages and dump them in the river; nothing she could do when she was told to dispose of her older brother the same way. The soldiers had argued among themselves, she recalled, about whether to kill her brother or Koma herself; they had been upset, it seemed, by the suspicion that they planned to escape. Or perhaps that hadn't been the reason. In Koma's telling, events simply occurred; reasons and even sequences of events were hard to reach, no matter how many times we spoke, no matter what translator I used to make my questions more intelligible. They had chosen her brother instead of her. They had leaned him against a tree, made certain that she watched. "He tell me goodbye," she remembered. "He say go tell mommy they go kill me. And then they fire. The head scatter."

She pulled the body to the water. She had asked to bury it in the forest instead. To leave him in the river, to be eaten by crocodiles and fish, was sacrilege; if she could only cover him with leaves . . . She had no more choice in this than in anything else. "If you cry," she said, of the time she was held down and the "RUF" initials carved across her breasts, "they go shoot you. And when they work go done, you tell thank you." Not only to the carvers—she approached the unit's top commander to express her gratitude. And she sang the anthem:

> *R.U.F. is fighting to save Sierra Leone*
> *R.U.F. is fighting to save our people*

Around her they took children from their mothers, hacked them in half and left the sections strewn beside the path. At least her baby was still alive. She related all this without tears or a tone of self-pity, as though endurance had been, and still was, the only option. "When they want you they take you," she said, and two men had, Colonel Danger and a man named Bad Breeze. She was pretty, with smooth skin and clear eyes and a strong smile, maybe not pretty enough to be chosen and protected by a top commander, but fortunate to be shared by Danger and Bad Breeze rather than being raped by anyone who felt the desire.

And all this was witnessed by the baby boy she'd carried from the start in the cloth pouch on her back, until Koma's scarred breasts, underfed, quit producing enough milk, and Dura cried too often. "When they kill they say laugh," she reported flatly, and described Colonel Danger holding the baby, dragging a bayonet across the throat and jabbing the blade into chest and belly, then placing the boy in Koma's arms, blood pooling in her hands, and commanding her to carry out one more river burial.

It would have seemed fantastic, anywhere else. Here what felt implausible was that after everything she'd lived through, everything she'd been made to accept, she had any volition left at all, any will to escape or to mold a future. But she had fled when rebel factions had fought each other, and now, at the center, she hoped to learn to dye cloth, to produce *lappas* with local indigo, and to learn enough arithmetic to launch her own business.

"This is my mansion on a hill," Mary said of the building where Koma went to class. The grand two-story house stood above Kabala, a town whose walls, having suffered seventeen invasions and battles, had crumbled to a low, roofless outline of homes, engulfed by bushes and young trees, the greenery of war. In what houses and hovels remained, the people lived along unpaved streets that turned to riverbeds in the rainy season, cataracts churning. The school hovered 200 feet up a hillside, suspended between the town and the ring of mist that, some mornings, encircled an adjacent rocky crest like a halo. But looked at a certain way, the building really wasn't all that grand, and it definitely wasn't a mansion. It was merely plain and hulking, with four or five rooms upstairs, two or three simple balconies, a minimal bathroom. Only against its surroundings did it become astonishing.

A few months earlier, it had belonged to those surroundings, an oversized version of everything below. Its owner, the widow of a politician, had abandoned it, and though it had somehow escaped the war's worst destruction, it had been left to disintegrate, its ceilings rotted to bare rafters, its windows, without shutters or glass, nothing but gaping wounds, its rooms alive with the smell of bat dung, an odor so heavy and sweet that in the hothouse air it was hard not to gag. Where the ceilings remained, the animals beat their wings in the dark vaults between wood and metal sheeting, a militia of hundreds.

The mission had rented the house and paid for the renovation, but it was Joseph, wiry, resourceful, his smile made charming by a slight overbite, who had made it happen. The Kortenhovens, trying to "facilitate" or "animate" as it was called in development circles, to nurture local capability and leadership, had left the renovation to him, while they finished up programs in Freetown. As a nine- or ten-year-old boy in the 1960s, Joseph had offered to help carry a neighbor's chickens out of their village, in the hope of seeing his first car at a distant junction. The desire had driven his legs many more miles than he or his parents had planned, until at last he'd not only seen but gotten to ride in a truck—and found himself in a far-off town with no way home. There he'd begun teaching himself to read with the help of schoolboys at the Catholic compound. Years later he'd cobbled together an education in agriculture, partly by borrowing the books of university students he happened to meet. With the Kortenhovens' mission, he'd been trying to improve Kuronko methods in rice, palm, and cassava farming; now, for the women's school, he was put in charge of hiring the contractor from Freetown and directing the work. And any time I lost my bearings, my despair growing to the point that Borthwick's words—"They can't do anything without the white man standing over them"—seemed almost reasonable, I had only to think of the transformation Joseph managed. Three months after Mary had chosen the wreck as the most likely building for a school, he showed her a place that, in the context of Kabala, was nothing less than a castle. The outside walls were a brilliant white, the windows were filled with mullioned glass, and the dark wood paneling in the downstairs rooms, a strange and extravagant feature that had seemed, before, only to add to the gloom, was newly stained and glossed and spoke vaguely of opulence, as though the school might educate royalty rather than girls like Koma.

A half-circle of stone tile had been laid before the front steps, beds of special white flowers—said to repel snakes—had been planted in back, and white-painted rocks formed the borders of a carport. Upstairs, the ceilings were all silent, the smell vanished. It seemed the militia of bats had never existed.

The school, it turned out, would be the Kortenhovens'

legacy. Around the time it opened, the Christian Reformed Church sent word of a decision, that Mary and Paul's mission was complete, that within a year they would have to return home, home to Grand Rapids, Michigan, if home was home any longer. It was time to test whether their work could be carried on by Sierra Leoneans like Joseph, and like Robert Jawara, a reserved, dignified man who would head the mission as it became locally run. This had been the goal all along, the end Mary and Paul had been aiming for since 1980: self-reliance for the people they had set out to rescue.

But for the Kortenhovens it was happening too quickly. "I'm just a little bit angry," Mary said, voice steady, straightforward—there remained only hints of the shy Calvin College graduate whose parents couldn't imagine her surviving a year's posting in Africa. "The church is going to abandon Sierra Leone the same way everyone abandons Africa. They've grown tired of it. It's worn them down." At the far end of town from the school, she talked by lantern-light in the mission's Kabala office, a cell furnished with a few wobbly chairs. "Well, can't they see that this is the time to really accomplish something? You don't wait through an entire war and then give up the minute it might be over. You don't let everything to go waste."

As part of the shift to local leadership, the church would be cutting its funding, paying the salaries of Robert and Joseph, but paying for fewer and fewer projects, so that money would have to be solicited from international agencies. This had always been true to a degree, and Paul had been adept at penetrating the bureaucracies of the U.N. or the European Union, and at finding more improbable sources. (The renovation for the school was paid partly by the U.N. and partly by the American actress and *Tomb Raider* star Angelina Jolie, who had somehow heard of the Kortenhovens' work through the U.S. ambassador.) But with the shift, the need for non-church money would soon become complete, and what contacts, what skills would the Sierra Leoneans have for handling the world of expatriate donors? Paul had been trying to teach the arts of writing grant proposals and cultivating funders; still, he and Mary were afraid that Robert and Joseph weren't ready. (And later, when the year's transition was over and the Kortenhovens had gradually stood back entirely, they would tell me that reports to the U.N. were delayed, starting to jeopardize support for the school.) "I worry," she said, voice quavering in the lantern-light, "that the ability for long-range planning just isn't there yet."

Two decades of work might amount to nothing. For in Foria, and in much of the Kuronko region their mission had covered, the increments of progress they'd brought had been largely wiped out during the war: water pipes had been vandalized and left useless; farms had shrunk for lack of seed programs to supplement war-diminished yields; immunization campaigns had been impossible; the birthing kits, with their scissors and plastic mats, had been looted; a little health clinic and dispensary they'd built in Foria was rubble. So much of the past was already gone. And now the future, the school, could easily collapse, the project one last sign of futility. "We need more time, at least another two years." Mary's body was so motionless and straight in her rickety chair that I almost didn't see her tears.

In the barren office with the lantern guttering, amidst the lightless town, it was easy to envision the students replaced by the bats, the sound of their wings and the smell of their dung.

One morning school began with a lecture on AIDS. Next to the mansion, in an open-sided outbuilding, the hundred students had gathered for assembly, crowded on long benches, a few suckling the babies the war had given them. A woman from Kabala named Sister Princess stood up front in a jerri curl wig and warned against the ways the disease could be caught: the "chook" of a needle used to sculpt hair; the cut of an old razor used for ritual markings or circumcision; sex if the boyfriend "na jump jump," if he had more than one partner, and if the woman didn't insist on a "one-foot sock," a condom. Theresa Kargbo, the administrator of the school, had written and taught the women a song, and they broke into hymn-like chorus for Sister Princess:

Come let us use the condom
When the man is ready
When the penis is ready
Oh let us use the condom

It was a sex education program as modern as any for its frankness. Sister Princess then asked what should be done for anyone who had the disease.

"Kill them," came the response.

After Sister Princess suggested avoidance instead, "Na put them on side," the condom hymn was repeated, and then Mary rose to speak, wearing a denim skirt and white T-shirt. "God done give you dis chance," she said quietly, standing with a measure of self-effacement to the side of the assembly. "Let you hold yourself fine. Let you hold each other fine. The way you go hold the next one, so God hold you. Let people look to you as one fine example."

Anger and worry showed nowhere on her face. Today she seemed to trust that all would not be wasted, that when she and Paul had gone, the school would go on gaining strength.

The women went in for class. Koma carried a bedraggled test booklet filled with problems she'd copied off the board, sum after sum. Soon she would be taught *gara*, the art of stitching fabric into special coils, dipping it in vats of indigo, and releasing the coils to reveal splendid patterns of rich blue-black; the art of making the indigo itself, mixing leaves and roots in a process that stretched over five days; the art of creating a suede-toned dye, with a gold tint like a lion's mane, from the grindings of kola nuts. Soon, the plan went, she would sell her fabrics in town. Never mind that Kabala's market sold little more than boiled eggs and flip-flops. Never mind that the sixty-cent flip-flops were an item to be saved for. Never mind that to make even a tiny profit on the cloth, after all the expenses were added up, the women would have to charge about eight dollars per piece, a price beyond the reach of nearly everyone in town except the mission's staff. This problem of basic economics would somehow be worked out. "Mother Mary will know what to do," the *gara* teacher said.

In the meantime the women had to learn basic math to carry out their businesses. Koma's class had just begun subtraction. The students giggled as they were called up to the board by a local teacher in one of the wood-paneled rooms. "Six minus five equals box," the teacher said, drawing the empty box awaiting the answer, and though she drilled the students in this robotic way for an hour, they never lost interest. "Put six mangoes together," she instructed, and the students drew six ovals in the booklets. "Now pull five mangoes. How much mangoes it go equal?" The first two women beckoned to the board failed to solve the equation. But the third, getting it right, danced in the aisle as her classmates applauded.

The teacher made things easier. "Two minus one equals box." She called on Koma, who stepped to the front of the room in her "If You Don't Practice . . . You Don't Deserve to Dream" T-shirt, took the chalk from the teacher's hand, and began to consider the problem. The room was hushed, as though everyone were deep in prayer.

THIRTEEN

The woman waving a red bandanna stood before a poster of 9/11. It was May 2002, and on the streets of Freetown the poster was still being sold, the montage of exploding towers, fleeing workers glazed in ash, apocalyptic clouds. This was the local version of the *Day of Tragedy* booklets, with their identical images, peddled from sidewalk tables outside my home, just by the World Trade Center. I can't say why the posters were popular. I never asked. I can only guess that the many reasons bore a pale yet plain resemblance to the reasons in New York. But I can say that the condolences offered me, as an American, were constant and, as best I could tell, shocked and sincere and weighted with empathy, here in this country unknown to so much of the world, this country of rubble, this nation whose capital streets, whose towns, whose villages were Ground Zero.

The woman waved furiously. Across the street, another shook a palm frond, green spears flailing. Elections had come! Peace had lasted! Disarmament was done! Democracy was taking hold! "Hot and bright! Hot and bright!" the woman with the red bandanna yelled the slogan of her party, and the other screamed back across the stalled nighttime traffic, "Wu teh-teh! Wu teh-teh!" which meant "Everything in abundance," the slogan of hers. The waving of cloth and leaves, of red and green, the rival party colors, grew more fierce, the shouting louder and more fanatic, and as shirtless teenagers in Santa Claus hats, backers of the red party, the All People's Congress, spilled from the shanties and ran in drunken mobs through the exhaust-clogged air, and as teenage platoons of green, from Kabbah's Sierra Leone People's Party, clustered everywhere, and as no one be-

lieved all the guns had been turned in, a part of me waited for
riot, for gunfire.

But there was nowhere to go. Up ahead, a board of nails had
been set in front of a van whose driver hadn't paid some kind of
dues or extortion. A sudden court was convened, collectors and
driver raging and shoving. No vehicle could move. There was
nothing to do but lean back and inhale the lingering exhaust of
ancient engines, thick and acrid enough that it scarcely dissi-
pated as ignitions were turned off. There was nothing to do as
the boys in floppy hats with jingly bells and white fluff drummed
on car hoods and blew red whistles, and as more in red Chicago
Bulls jerseys bearing Michael Jordan's 23, and in red rags tied
Jesse James–style across the lower halves of their faces, sang out,
demanding, "Kabbah where de diamond?" and as a cacophony
of "Wu teh-teh"s rose in reply—nothing to do but believe that no
street-fighting would erupt, that the only thing erupting here
was democracy, in all its new energy and anarchic spirit, in all
the exuberance of a population given its voice. Maybe it was
even true that all the shouting back and forth was as much celebration as dispute. It felt good to believe that, and it didn't feel
ridiculously far-fetched. Red swarmed through the cars and
green cried out from the roadside and nothing happened. But
there in the dark, where the only glimmers came from the can-
dles of women selling mangoes on the ground, I could imagine
the boys in Santa hats wielding axes and machetes.

And where the pink whistles of the People's Liberation Party
started to blow, more than a few in the mob surely had done
some cutting. This was Johnny Paul Koroma's crew, his government troops having butchered their way through Lamin's neighborhood three years ago. Some danced across the road in
women's wigs. "J.P.!" they bellowed. "J.P.!" One gyrated in cow-
boy boots and short-short cutoffs slit up the sides. "Satan is gone
and Johnny Paul is here!" Marijuana wafted through the air. "We
are soldiers," they declared, and yelled Koroma's nickname:
"Angel! Angel! Angel!" One man, looking almost rabid with

drugs or democracy or the sheer overheated surge of the crowd, wanted to make sure I understood something: "If people say we cut arms, is not true!" They were certain Kabbah would steal the election, and waved photocopies of an old Freetown newspaper page, or hand-scrawled signs with just its headline. From a few years ago, it told of army officers being executed. "More to Die," the signs declaimed.

"Organization for the Survival of Mankind," the R.U.F. had named its civil wing, as it had turned in weapons and turned itself into a political party, the R.U.F.P. "Our flag symbol," one leader told me (with Foday Sankoh still imprisoned, said to be badly ill and delusional, under a wild profusion of white dreadlocks), "is a cool, laying down, very calm lion." Bottles and rocks and sticks flew between the boys of the palm fronds and the boys of the prone lion. But bloody faces and scalps were the worst of what happened in the week reeling up to voting, and waking long before dawn on election day, ducking shoulders into canvas straps, tugging socks up to biceps and pulling on plastic casing, then dressing with his two-fingered steel hands, Lamin walked uphill to the locked gates of his polling place.

"Yes, sah! Thank you, sah!" people called wherever they saw British soldiers. On the ground and just offshore, the British were gradually cutting their troops from what had been a thousand toward what would be one or two hundred, and though they promised their commitment would never fade, it was easy to think, with the war in Afghanistan and the threat of war in Iraq, and with the initial exuberance of this mission long ago worn off, that a fading away had already begun. Yet among the Sierra Leoneans, the British retained an omnipresent and omnipotent aura, perhaps because the old talk of a 5,000-man "over the horizon" force, a particular horizon and force no one had ever actually seen, still hovered comfortingly in civilian minds, or perhaps because the remaining soldiers seemed to guarantee U.K. onslaught if peace deteriorated, or perhaps because even a few hundred British troops felt like a hundred thousand of their own. Whatever the magic, the thanks were plainly deserved. Their presence was the mainstay, keeping things stable enough to make this attempt at elections. (And the U.K. meant to increase its non-military teams, starting with one to revive the judiciary; to add to its advisors, its quasi-cabinet to the president, trying to establish patterns of "good governance"; and to keep its top brass superintending the army, assuming Kabbah won the vote as expected, or that whoever did was amenable.) "Without the British," Corinne Dufka said, "this show is over."

But she didn't support everything they were doing, and sometimes they didn't seem easy with the programs they'd fallen into. Colonel Jonny Lowe looked over a selection camp, then said to me, "You wouldn't see this in the Balkans, I can tell you." Around him stood disarmed troops, R.U.F. and Civil Defense Forces. In the camp, the enemies had been living in the same cramped tents, even wedging themselves onto the same narrow platforms to sleep. Blue eyes filled with warmth and bewilderment, Lowe gestured toward the men, who sang together as they lined up. "You get the feeling in the Balkans that nothing is going to change. The bitterness runs too deep. Here, now, they're playing football together, and last week they could have been cutting each other's throats, and cutting whatever else."

Because no one could figure out what to do with all the rebel and hunting society gunmen turning in their weapons, because there weren't any jobs to keep them from returning to war, the British had decided to send as many as possible into the new Sierra Leone Army. They ran them through a perfunctory screening interview—"to placate humanitarian fears" as one officer put it, fears that huge numbers of war criminals, especially ex-R.U.F., were being given better guns and taught to better use them—and then took them on for training.

The British knew the army would be bloated; they knew their own government, which had agreed to pay the extra S.L.A.

salaries, wouldn't back this kind of program forever; and they knew that these very soldiers, among the most volatile of all, would probably be the first few thousand to be cut from the ranks. "On the other hand," Lowe said, after marveling at the tranquility in the tents, the harmony of the singing—created, it seemed, merely by the promise of regular pay—"they might just as easily turn back into the lunatics they were." But the British felt they had no alternative. They would prevent war now and pray hard later.

An element of faith in the ability—and desire—of the country's gunmen to change their ways had always been part of the British approach. This went along with the mission's acceptance of its own muddled morality, an acceptance that could seem, by turns, sophisticated or cynical or oblivious, either a necessary flaw, the product of realistic thinking, or an ill-advised shortcut, born of willful or innocent ignorance. From the start, the British had been training and equipping government troops who'd never been anywhere close to reliable, taking the risk that, when they left, they would have empowered the next coup. They'd been trying to mold the future with men partially responsible for the worst of the nation's past. This was true not only at the low and anonymous levels, but at ranks that were high and conspicuous. Until his alleged coup-plotting brought him down, one top-ranking Sierra Leonean soldier sat in a well air-conditioned office at the S.L.A. headquarters the British oversaw. According to some from around Kabala, the man had led a unit that made a habit of pulverizing babies to death with a rice mortar and pestle.

Many in the lower ranks, meanwhile, passed through the British courses, swore their loyalty to the civilian government, and still clung to the leadership of Johnny Paul Koroma, perhaps ready to follow his orders or those of his seconds, men like C. O. Gullit, who'd once taken me to see the old West Side Boys base where Major Marshall and the other British captives had been held. To get there, we'd ridden in a shallow dugout canoe;

we seemed to sit on the surface of the water, gliding atop the glassy river past two young, half-naked fisherwomen. Their nets made a faint splashing sound. Our oarsman's paddle, with its diamond-shaped blade, made no sound at all. Gullit, in a blue jeans suit and aviator shades, sucked on morale boostahs and tutored me in the reasons he and his renegade government soldiers had emerged from the jungle to storm the capital three years ago: "If the army cannot intervene to solve the problems of the country, it is not an army."

"We asked the consent of the civilians," he added, as I thought of the cutting, torching, and raping. "We are using the Geneva Convention."

I often went to those hills, just outside the capital, where the devastation had been heaviest. People laughed when I asked whether they ever saw the soldiers who'd hacked and burned through their neighborhoods now soldiering as members of the British-made army—they laughed at the naivete of the question. They did see them, of course, and treated them warily. Some doubted such men could ever be remade; some believed the British could work that magic as well. But I heard no one criticize what the British were doing.

It was like that with Lamin. I'd heard that C. O. Cut Hands, or Sahjunior, was in the new S.L.A. Two of Lamin's old neighbors, as well as Sahjunior's aunt, said they'd seen him in uniform around the city. I never succeeded in tracking him down to confirm this, but Lamin had heard the same, and sometimes he talked about what would happen if they met up.

"Maybe someone will scratch me and say, This is the man that has done the atrocity to you. And then I will just go to him. I will just say, Man, see what you have done. You have left me to be a handicap. I will tell him, You will not remain on this earth for one hundred or two hundred years. One day you will have to go. You must be recalled by your master, the Maker, to give account of what you have done with me.

"Of course, I will not feel fine within my heart at that moment when he is facing me. But if I take my revenge on him, it will not make my hands grow back."

I asked about the fact that C. O. Cut Hands might have gone through British training and be again in the army.

"Well," Lamin answered, "that has been determined by the international community." Clearly it didn't please him, but for all his sharpness of thought, he spoke as though even to consider such things was far beyond him. He spoke with resigned trust, as though, for the country, this were the only way.

And maybe it would all work out. Maybe the British were wrong, not about their approach but in their dejection, their dismal sense of the future, their minimal view of their own accomplishment, their feeling, as Borthwick had described it, that "when we go, it will be like taking your hand out of a bucket of water." For even with the coming of elections, Colonel Lowe, with his tentative and bewildered note of hope, was the exception. The dominant mood was that of the police chief, Keith Biddle, whose boundless energy again gave way in a moment of contemplation, whose long body again went listless as he allowed himself to settle in the soft furniture of his office (for a few minutes, anyway, before he sprang up, saying there was work to do and chasing me out), who laughed—the laughter of a man who feels there is no other recourse—as he talked again of corruption, of the "malaise and lack of urgency" that surrounded him, enveloped him. One of his British task force put in that he thought election day would come off without significant trouble. Biddle acknowledged that "a lot of people thought we'd never get this far." Those were his only words of progress. He talked of all the times he prayed, "Beam me up, Scotty," and, asked to assess the country's future, pursed his thin lips below his formidable nose, exhaled in a puff that left his face utterly slack, and mumbled, "I'm not optimistic."

But wasn't there a place for optimism? To step back, to see

things from a distance, was sometimes to feel there was. Two years ago, when I'd started traveling to Sierra Leone, the safe zone in the country had barely reached outside Freetown. Now I could head out to Koidu, all the way east, without thinking twice. In the war's most contested region, things had grown almost orderly since my last visit. The diggers had pulled their picks and sifters back from the town, agreeing not to mine there, to minimize the risk of feuds and digger wars during election week. The U.N. troops were patrolling without fear, smiling from the tops of their armored personnel carriers. The homesick Pakistani battalion, who treasured a tented museum, a shrine of delicate Pakistani ceramics and painted camel-skin lampshades, of jeweled daggers and hats and Pakistani volleyballs ("the world's best volleyballs," a captain had told me) within their military compound, had even ventured out to construct a playground for Koidu's children. Between collecting golden lakes of surrendered bullets, and sledge-hammering and sawing relinquished guns, the peacekeepers had built tire swings and climbing bars and painted, across a wall, a giant Donald Duck sitting on a big red heart.

The Sierra Leoneans were optimistic. Some were rejoicing. True, there were skeptics, people planning to lay low, keep out of harm's way on voting day. "In Sierra Leone," a man warned me, "we could mess up a wet dream." But in a country of five million, two and a half million had made sure to register. Impromptu bands of revelers formed in the streets, tooting low, playful notes with a kind of bassoon-like wooden tube and shaking maracas made from rusty cans. People bought new batteries for their transistor radios, to be certain they could hear the results, and those who could write invested in extra pens, planning to keep a running tally of votes, polling station by polling station, as they were announced. Foday, driving at dusk along the beach where the infinite tiny fish shimmered in the huge nets like mounds of silver coins, said, "Last year, I had in my mind always—they burn my mother, son, my car. These things . . .

Now, it's more clear." Once, he'd expressed an opinion I'd heard elsewhere in other ways, "You can't rule Africa like you rule Europe," that democracy couldn't work; if he couldn't have British rule, he would hope for a beneficent local dictator. But these days, with the wooden tubes giving out their happy, song-less notes like tremendous party favors, he didn't seem so worried.

Yet this would have been the most hopeful thing: an end to the wish for British control; that longing gone with the coun-try's diminished desperation; peace allowing for nascent self-confidence. There were faint signs. Sidi Conteh, the gentle, well-composed man who was Foday's boss, said, "If the British rule, we have shame. Our president must be a black man. We must govern ourselves. I like the British to head our institutions. The head of the army. The head of the civil service. The head of any important institution, I would like that. The only thing I would not welcome is that the white man be president. That must be a black. To show we are a country and we are able to co-ordinate our own affairs." He would vote for Kabbah, he ex-plained as many did, partly because he worked well with the international community in getting aid, and partly because "he has a white attitude," which meant, in Sidi's view, that "he obeys the rule of law," that he was a leader who did not steal.

Abdul Tejan-Cole, stepping from the sanctuary of his law of-fice, down broken stairs, through a refuse-strewn alley, and on toward the elaborate colonial court building, newly renovated by the British, didn't share the prevailing racial reverence. Walking by the market stalls in his dark suit, he had impeccable grace, and when he spoke it was with the easy self-assurance of all his education, here, in Britain, in the States. But passing under the classical statues that guarded the building's archway, pulling on the British-style wig, with its hemp-tinted curls, still worn in courtrooms here, and sitting in his robe and black string tie, un-der the lethargic ceiling fan, waiting for the judge's uncertain ar-rival, he lamented an imprisonment: Only expatriate money could supply the law library Sierra Leone didn't have (Abdul had to photocopy any case he wanted a judge to consider) or the court reporters who were nowhere to be seen (judges had to record their own proceedings, scolding attorneys and witnesses to pause, to "Watch my pen!" until a point was written down) or enough prosecutors to make criminal justice a viable notion (there were right now only five for the entire country). Only contact with expatriate judges, he felt, a mingling and collaboration he hoped might come through the establishment of a special war crimes tribunal, could present the local judiciary with an alternative to the rule of bribery, the offerings of satellite dishes or tuition for a child's schooling abroad or any smaller token remotely affordable, that generally meant there was no reason to show up in court at all.

Down the street from the building, women selling fabric said the British should govern for at least ten years. But Lamin surprised me. His eyes did something quick, something I can't describe, a momentary shift and hardening maybe, when I asked if he still wished the British would take over. What he wished, clearly, was that he'd never said that. "I wanted them for rulers because everything was looking very much tedious." Now there was hope. Now "we will be pleased to have them for advice." And protection. But not to govern.

We had this conversation during a drive above the Bunce River, sunset turning the lagoons to purple silk, and after a while he began talking of other things, of how M-A had stood by him, how good she had been, then of how he'd first met her when she was a young "petty trader" twenty years ago, and how he'd saved so they could marry. I asked what had made him fall in love. And a minute later I was staring out the window again, to where, with night, the purple had turned to a broad river of emptiness.

"Well," he said, sounding almost surprised that I should need to ask, "you can see her color. She resembles as if she is a white woman. So I love her for that."

■ ■ ■

"I had a much stronger sense of God then, as a girl, in Foria," Sarah, Mary and Paul's daughter, had told me in Grand Rapids, where her parents would soon be returning. "I used to feel some sense of—eternity maybe?" she said in her modest house on her street of square lawns in her city of malls. "It's hard to describe, but I used to have these little moments lying in bed, listening to the sounds of the village. If it was a full moon night, everyone was up until one in the morning. I could hear kids playing or singing a song, and women beating rice with that rhythm, and sometimes one of the drummers played and girls danced . . ."

Her voice trailed off. She spoke for a bit, too, of being surrounded by the spirituality of the villagers, their constant sense of fate. Then she gave up trying to explain. She didn't mention beauty, but I heard it: the graceful curve of a vine bridge sweeping low above a river; the cotton trees with their giant buttresses, their chambers of unearthly embrace; the path that bent with elusive promise amidst the heartbreaking green. And I thought I knew something of what she was trying to evoke, thought I had experienced, here and there, in Sierra Leone and other countries, a small version of it: the transcendent feeling in the impossibly remote place, the gorgeous and impoverished place, the place of splendor and devastation where people were acutely aware of the size of the unknown and where every voice, every song, every drumbeat, every simple act like preparing a meal, seemed to carry along with it, in the immediate background, a religious hush if you listened in just the right way, and a comforting hint of God.

Yet comforting possibilities felt obliterated by Lamin's words. "So I love her for that." Such a fundamental self-hatred seemed to speak of nothing but a desolate universe.

■ ■ ■

On election day, Komba walked happily through a cemetery. He wore his best and only long pants, the corduroys with the wales worn smooth, and a T-shirt drenched in sweat from his swift, excited strides. He'd been told to vote in one place, then told, when he reached there, to vote in another, two miles away. He didn't complain, just hurried off through the graves, clutching his card in his right hand, with his name and registration number.

The night before, the rainy season had begun. It was as if I'd been underwater, completely submerged, within seven steps of dashing from my hotel room. The rain battered the city's metal roofs with such an unceasing roar that voices were inaudible. Even shouting didn't much work. I always forgot, one rainy season to the next, what Sierra Leone's deluges were like. They vanquished even the heat, chilled the skin. They were spectacular, seemed to promise to annihilate everything, to leave the world new.

But the season never arrived all at once. It teased, and as Komba crossed the vast cemetery the sky was a pale blue and the dirt had drunk all it received and turned back to a reddish dust. The gravestones were fallen or overgrown; the tops of tombs were missing, bushes thrusting from burial soil. Komba took no notice. He walked fast enough that it was hard to keep up. It wasn't late, only mid-morning, and the polls would stay open all day. But he wanted to get there. He was going to vote.

He had taken part in none of the rallies, worn no Santa hat, waved no palm frond, blown no whistle, hurled no rocks. He would have fit in with those packs well enough, certainly with the Organization for the Survival of Mankind or the throng crying "Angel!"—the crews that had kidnapped and raised him, fathered him and, later, been his boys. But now, if you needed your car fixed in the King Tom area of Freetown, you might easily have turned into a particular garage, and seen Komba leaning under a hood.

You couldn't have seen anything of his past. You wouldn't

have seen anything out of the ordinary, only a young man, perhaps nineteen, among six or seven other apprentices, without
tools, gazing longingly at engine parts, wishing they had the
equipment and knowledge to fix them. The garage boss had little incentive to train them. He valued the grunt work they did,
the sucking of a bit of gas—lips to a scrap of tubing—whenever a
car was brought in for service, so there would be fluid to clean
the motor. He valued, with Komba, the payments he got for taking him on. The yard was jammed with forsaken vehicles to practice on. (They'd been used overseas to the Western definition of
uselessness, shipped for resale here, where definitions were different, and left, in the end, to die in the garage, when tape and
hand-rigged parts were no longer enough and foreign ones were
unaffordable.) But the boss offered his teaching, and the chance
to practice with his wrenches, at rare intervals. The education
had the pace of a spiritual journey, led by a charlatan. Once each
month, maybe, he imparted the workings of a single component.
At this rate, Komba could declare himself a mechanic in about a
decade. So far, he was sticking with it. More than a year had
passed, and most days I went to look for him, he was there, waiting to learn.

Yet how much longer would his patience hold?—especially
with the dream at the far end, to be a mechanic, so meager: little
more than subsistence living on a farm of rust. "When it rain
cold in bush, there is war," he'd said of the future, a few months
ago. Peace couldn't hold out forever against poverty. It was akin
to what Foday had said: "Where there is no money, there is no
human being." But for now Komba said his own past was finished, and he spoke of the baby he'd just had with a refugee
girl newly returned from Guinea. Beneath his high, wide,
scarred cheekbones, he smiled as he told me he'd named the
baby Hawa after his mother, whom he'd last seen when he'd
been taken, and begun living in a roving orphanage of blood
and flame.

At his polling station, two hours went by and somehow the

lines gave no hint of forward movement. The courtyard was without trees. People clung to the low building, in a thin strip of shadow. Komba scraped his thumb across his forehead, raking pools of sweat. Shoving began. Voices climbed. Komba was in the thick of it. Then, in a moment, the disruption ceased. The line straightened itself. Stillness returned. The voters would wait until any problem inside—over the checking of the handwritten registration sheets or over the correct folding of the paper ballots—was fully resolved, until everything was exactly right, perfectly fair, held no excuse for trouble. I cannot tell you that they all knew what democracy was. When I asked Komba, he dropped his head and said softly, "That is the problem." But I can say that they had assembled not only to vote for their different candidates. They had come to vote, unanimously, against history, and there might have been no limit to how long they would wait for that. The aura of patience they gave out made me think of Michael's word: Herculean.

With his kind, bearish face, his broad shoulders, his pincered hands, Lamin stood at the iron gates, having emerged as chief, mayor, and shepherd to the amputees lined up before him. "Pa Jusu!" they called to him with their worries. "Pa Jusu!" He wore blue jeans, a sportshirt of faded but still cheerful yellow-and-blue plaid, and, instead of the new boots he liked to put on for a sense of solidity and position in the world, a pair of run-down sandals with a fake buckle on the side, put on for the needs of this historic day.

"Because that he does not want me to die," his daughter Hannah had said, "neither to go astray, he lost his hands." He had saved her life, saved her from being raped, urged her out the back window, pushed her up by the hips when she couldn't climb out herself, then returned to the front door, to the soldier's wrath. "But when I saw him without hands, I did not even know that he was my father."

After her escape, she had cowered in another house, somehow concealing herself into the next day, hearing the soldiers crying through the neighborhood, "Come out and feel de breeze! Feel free! Feel free!" Her mother had found her, managed to get her to the yard of the surgeon's shack. There the amputees and other wounded lay on the ground, untended by the shack's owner, but at least left alone by the soldiers, who seemed to feel they were well-enough ruined. "My conscious was not at that time correct," she remembered. "I did not recognize him. I was not conscious properly."

She laughed briefly, timidly, with deep unease at the memory. Her large eyes were lovely. Her slender face was beautiful. She wasn't crying. She'd lived with this too long for tears. She said she thought of what had happened every day. But many times as she spoke, she smiled or laughed uncomfortably, with disbelief and, I sensed, a great deal of shame at what she'd failed to do: Once she'd realized who he was, she didn't hold him. She didn't touch him. She didn't cry.

"I was unconscious. I was so confused. When you are walking you see somebody with a baby lying on the ground, dead, some other ones burned with the tire around the neck. The breast was cut and the baby was alive. And the next woman she's pregnant with her stomach opened. I was scared. A dog was eating her stomach where they tore it. I was just mixed up."

She had thought, too, that "he would be receiving his hands again, his body would make new hands."

Only later, as the soldiers had shifted farther from the city, and as she and Lamin and M-A joined an exodus toward downtown, had she cried. It happened when Lamin, staggering, fell. His friends wept as they lifted him to his feet. Finally her father's weakness overwhelmed her.

And now she and Lamin never talked seriously of what had happened. They never had. But he offered her the comfort of small jokes. Sometimes, if he was composing a long letter, he would ask her to copy it out for him, because of her fine handwriting. "Lend me your hand," he would say. Or, "Give me your hand." And telling me of this, she laughed again quickly, not with shame but with the pleasure of having her father's love.

What if they had lost their registration card? What if they couldn't fold the ballot? The amputees from his camp needed to know they would still be let in, that their votes would still be counted. Lamin assured them they would. It was dawn, the gates about to be unlocked, the polling station to open. He found a scrap of paper and demonstrated the folding against his thigh. "In fact," he promised, "there are people in there, sensitized, to show you how to do."

By a kind of informal camp council, he'd been asked to be camp chairman after the last man was accused of embezzling what few donations came in to help the residents. He'd taken over the cube of an office, forty feet from the latrines. He opened the padlock nimbly every day. Behind his table, clean of everything except his carefully placed black briefcase, or sitting on a bench outside if the office grew insufferably hot, he heard the disputes of the camp, sat as arbitrating judge. A woman complained that her husband beat their daughter too severely. The man stood to demonstrate what he'd done: "I slap," he said, making the motion with his remaining hand. "I kick, kick. Eh, Mr. Jusu, if I no beat me peekin, I no trainah." Lamin didn't entirely disagree, but warned the man to tone it down, that if he injured the girl badly he would need to pay for the doctor.

Between arbitrations he had a resettlement to handle. A Norwegian aid group was building a new camp fifteen miles outside the city. It would be less squalid than the current one, with two-room dwellings of concrete instead of shanties, but it would also be more isolated. On the hill above the lagoons, the amputees would be more vulnerable in any outbreak of war or rush of assaults and looting. Lamin was busy arranging a delegation to the nearest U.N. battalion, to make certain the new camp would be patrolled.

His own house-building was stalled. The two-story plans had been aborted at part of one story; what structure there was enclosed raw spaces. He'd put up a steel front door, a crucial luxury, for he felt that if he'd had a steel door the first time, rather than a wooden one that could be smashed through, he might have left it locked and stayed behind it—to think of this was to imagine everything different from the way it was. The door was the last addition he could afford. He hoped the novelist in New York would someday send him more money.

He hoped as well to return to the United States. In his plastic briefcase with the beige label that read "Sky Lucky," he kept his daughter Rugiatu's report card (six "excellent"s and two "very good"s), a soggy pad of lined paper, and his passport. He wanted me to contact the CIA. He wanted me, at least, to get him the agency's address. By working for the organization he would be able to live in America. "I can be employed there. I can be a perfect spy. People will not know me. They will say he is an amputee and not know me."

Meanwhile he gave inspiriting talks to tent cities of refugees, showing them how he could dress, flick the snaps of his briefcase, shave. And soon he would be trying to organize his camp to lobby for more government support, and trying, with the help of a local computer programmer, to create a website, to campaign, through whatever Western publicity he could attract, for compensation from the diamond industry for its acceptance of illicit gems that had helped fund the war.

A man with one crutch and one leg wanted to know how much time until the voting started. The sun had been up for a while now; the great crowd of camp residents had gathered in the dark; the man couldn't stand much longer. "Come up!" Lamin ushered him and others like him closer to the front. "Come up!"

A policeman opened the gates a sliver. The first ten in line were let through. On the wide dirt courtyard was a resilient flight of stairs climbing to the entrance of a fallen building, some U.N. soldiers in their light blue helmets, the school where the voting would take place, and the dozen or so journalists who'd appeared for the event. CNN had sent a team. This was a rare stop, their first in the country in two years. (Their story would get a few minutes, wouldn't even air, they said, in the United States.) Most of the Western newspapers didn't send reporters much more often. But a photo-op took shape. The ten hadn't been let through to vote; the polls weren't ready. An old mango tree stood alone in the middle of the courtyard. The amputees, Lamin among them, aligned themselves under it. The roots spread long and gnarled above the ground.

All posed for the cameras, some with empty faces, others euphoric. Several held up their voting cards. Lamin positioned his card in front of his right thigh, posing somberly with his right foot extended. Then he smiled, almost dancing, shaking that foot in the air.

"I am Lamin Jusu Jarka, chairman of the Murray Town amputees," he told the reporters over and over. To me, the tree haunted the scene, but I'm not sure he was aware of it, or if he was, that he cared. He was too caught up in the attention, elated and made half-frantic by it. "I am Lamin Jusu Jarka, chairman of the Murray Town amputees!" He knew how soon we would all be leaving.

Suddenly the throng of victims and their families stormed through the gates. They overpowered the policeman, who'd opened the bolt to let someone in or out; they drove at the iron doors, ran into the courtyard, some tripping and spilling, stumps scraping the ground. The photo-op was ended, everyone scurrying. But the throng settled itself quickly enough. They only wanted to vote. "Make line A!" Lamin directed everyone, after checking that his mother and M-A were safe. "Line A for this side, line B for this side!"

And at last it began. Lamin stepped into the schoolroom, where light crept through low windows. A poll worker in a fancy mauve dress and curlicue wig searched for Lamin's name on her pages. At the next table he rolled up the right pants leg of his jeans. The ballots were intended to be marked with a thumbprint. He slipped his foot from his sandal. A woman brushed the nail of his big toe with dark stain, to prevent him from voting twice. He turned toward a booth. It was a sort of collapsible cardboard podium with a little rim around the platform for privacy. With his fingers he lifted a disk, a circular ink pad, from the platform, set it on the floor, placed his glossy white ballot beside it. He pressed his big toe into the ink and pressed it again next to his candidate. Then he slid the folded paper into a translucent plastic tub, where it lay visible, blurry, gone.

"Daniel," he had called to me, as he'd stepped into the schoolroom. Somehow I'd let myself be distracted, and he'd waited until I caught up, not wanting me to miss his voting. Now it was over. He stood in front of me, but already I could feel him at the vanishing point.

FOURTEEN

Michael and I drove upcountry for an audience with Dr. Gebau. Along the way, out near Bo in the southeast, he wanted to take a detour. His mother's ancestral village was reached by no road at all, only a path climbing between forest and charred fields cleared for farming. While he hugged and talked with his mother, her upper body dusty and bare, I glanced around the mud dwellings. Yellow plastic jerricans, heavy with palm oil to be hauled out to market, were among the few signs of the modern world.

Whenever I felt most deeply my separation from the people of Sierra Leone, whenever I felt the dull-edged pain of my own limitations, Michael, with his Latin names for microorganisms and his plans for spectacular cures, offered me a way closer. He stood on a middle ground, and always I felt better to be with him. The middle ground was an island of visions and promise.

As we headed toward the doctor, Michael's most revered Kamajor priest, Michael's benefactor, Neall, muddled around his office beside the helipad. On the wall were detailed maps once used for planning strikes and supply drops, and taped next to the maps was a poem:

If you're not
Handsome at 20
Strong at 30
Wise at 40
Rich at 50
Forget it. You are finished.

These days, more than ever, he may have felt that way, finished. Kabbah's victory had been announced, and though there were accusations of fraud, of more votes than registered voters in Kabbah strongholds, and though the crowd at his own outdoor victory party had been too drunk and manic, too menacing in its joy, for him to risk emerging from his dark-windowed vehicle to speak, all had passed without violence. Across the helipad from the office, behind a single padlock, lay Neall's storeroom: the five-foot-long rockets packed in their wooden coffins, the sleek missiles kept in canisters that looked like an architect's drawing tubes, the chains of bullets with their thousands of black links that would fall through the sky, harmless as paper clips. It could be a long while before he needed any of it, before he was needed. Revolution had sparked up again in Liberia, with militias seeping into Sierra Leone to raid villages, with languishing Sierra Leonean fighters crossing the other way to find work. Guinea seemed barely stable. Only slightly farther away, the Ivory Coast, the most successful country in West Africa, was crumbling fast toward war. War could spill back into Neall's domain. As though trails of kerosene had been poured and lit from over the borders, all could explode. But for now his contract had been cut by a quarter; he worried about the Eastern Bloc pilots lurking around, sure they were willing to work for less and to kick back more; and, with his private air force sitting idle, he had little to do and none of his old adrenaline at all.

"I suppose I'll have to," he said, when I asked, one slow afternoon, if he could survive without the adrenaline, if he could get a decent night's sleep without the exhaustion that followed the rush. He laughed grimly at his needs, at the way he was made. He seemed to gird himself. "It's a question of adapting to circumstances."

He'd had offers. He talked of a call to hunt for bin Laden, an acquaintance putting together a team to go after the $25 million reward. There had been something, too, in the Comoros, nation of unending mercenary-led coups. "It would be nice to go out and shoot a bit," he said, and the thought seemed to reinject the possibility of pleasure into his always terse speech.

But he'd turned them down. The bin Laden hunt was beyond even his wish for danger; success, he figured, would mean being the most-sought prey of every jihadic soldier on earth. And then there was his eyesight, the sense of weakness because he wore glasses, because he now had such trouble hearing through the din of noisy bars, because he believed his concentration was slipping, caught himself distracted, even forgetful, and because he wondered, despite his saying no to the chance at bin Laden, whether he had any self-preserving judgment left to guide him in flight, any instinct at all for temporary retreat, or whether a career's worth of missions had worn that away.

It might be time, he thought. Younger men might make better pilots in war. He was close to trying what he'd tried before, to finding something "legitimate." He stopped on the word he'd spoken, smiled at himself for taking the perspective most people might take. What he did, he felt, *was* legitimate. Without him, the R.U.F. could well have had its turn in full power. Still, he could almost see forcing himself through the change.

He'd put a few thousand dollars into another mining venture, this time not with Lou, the Vietnam vet, but on his own. For now the machines were broken, but if he could raise a stake he thought he might start an eco-tourism business, buy a boat, build a fishing camp, take people out to the islands off the coast. The biggest tarpon ever caught in the world, he said, had been hooked off Sierra Leone. He didn't say it with much excitement.

His one other plan had nothing to do with employment. It had come in a strange way. A few months ago, Miss Sierra Leone had been terribly burned, allegedly by a jealous boyfriend. While she was still alive, her relatives had appeared one morning at Neall's door, begging cash for her treatment. He'd wound up starting a fund, raising money from a Freetown businessman, a local pop singer, a mobile phone company. Now he meant to raise more. He intended to build a burn center, something small, something realistic, but with a qualified staff, "because right now there isn't a place like that in the whole of Sierra Leone, nowhere a victim can go to get that type of treatment." As he imagined his clinic, his voice gave a sign of adrenaline.

Then, a few months later, an e-mail. The Ivory Coast was by that point tearing itself apart in battle. "Hoping for a possible contract," Neall wrote.

By lantern- and candlelight Michael and I sat with Dr. Gebau. Michael had wanted me to meet him, and had promised a demonstration of his powers, because he wished me to believe in the future he predicted. Two years ago, when I'd watched Commander Snake put on his proof, I'd felt little but curiosity and the thrill of the exotic. Those things were much less a part of it now. Something was at stake. I longed for the demonstration to be as glorious as Michael, his voice full of veneration and confidence, expected it to be.

Gebau, the second highest priest in all of Kamajor society, was a tall man in gray slacks and a loose red shirt with elaborate stitching. Blue suns rose from the waist and yellow patterns adorned the sleeves. But it was simply a pretty shirt; he made no show of amulets and mirrored pendants, let alone vipers, as Snake had. He looked to be around forty, with a gentle smile that came readily and a face where I could find no hint of self-doubt. He didn't seem at all worried about impressing me. Speaking in Mende with Michael translating, he said he regretted that disarmament had come; otherwise I could have witnessed his medicine against guns. But I would have plenty to see, he assured me, as we sat on his narrow veranda. In his yard, the cadaver of a car helped set him apart from destitution. He himself would only supervise, he said, as if taking part in an exhibition was of course beneath him, but his seven apprentices had been learning well, and I would not be disappointed by their abilities. From what he had taught them, I would understand how much more he himself could do.

Michael had not yet broached with the priest his desire to publicize Gebau's medical achievements worldwide—this, Michael would do in future years, once he had the academic qualifications to solidify his claims in the West—and so I couldn't ask Gebau what he thought of Michael's plans. But he clearly had great affection for Michael (if he hadn't, I, as an outsider, would never have come to sit so easily under the second high priest's corrugated eaves); it seemed he would be open to Michael's ideas. And as we talked before his apprentices began, he mentioned, without my asking, some of the diseases and ailments his mixtures, once blessed, could cure. He had purged all forms of insanity; restored the skin of people severely burned; eliminated cancer; overcome certain cases of AIDS. After a while, he brought out his attaché case to show me the leopard's tooth and sanctified white headcloth he kept inside. He also brought out his wooden staff. Sheathing its tip was a bullet casing, and carved at its head, just below the handle, was a highly detailed soldier equipped with grenades on his belt and cowries on his helmet. To have it out on the veranda was dangerous. Any woman who touched it would be paralyzed. In battle, holding the staff, he could spin around quickly, cry out "Oh, my mother," and make himself invisible. But I had only to wait. I would see. He was passing his gift on to others now.

Chests gleaming in kerosene light, the apprentices spread a raffia mat on the ground. Behind them were the silhouettes of a few low palms; above them was the powder of a sky strewn with stars; to the side was Gebau, watching serenely. A boy, maybe sixteen, maybe eighteen, stood alone on the mat, unwrapping razor blades from the packaging of thick paper they were sold in here.

"What are you seeing?" he asked. Michael and a few other onlookers stood or leaned a short distance away. The apprentices had motioned me to a chair, by itself, directly in front of the mat, as if to emphasize that I was the only one needing confirmation.

"Razor blades," I said.

Slight laughter rose at my obvious reply.

The boy took one of the blades between his fingers. He opened his mouth wide, put the blade in. I winced. "You don't have to do this," I said. I'd expected an obvious trick, like the one Snake had performed. But there was no denying the fact that a razor blade was in the boy's mouth.

He set it vertically at the back of his teeth, edges against molars, and clenched his jaw. The thirty seconds or so of chewing made a sound like a very noisy breakfast cereal. He swallowed and took up another blade, chewing again. He put in two at once. I was still wincing but wondering what the hoax could be. There were definitely no stores around, no Abracadabra Magic Shop in all of Sierra Leone, to buy fake razor blades. These were real. All I could think was that they'd been filed, yet the wrapping had looked crisp, not tampered with. I wanted to touch one of the blades, but they had all passed into the boy's esophagus on their way to his stomach. And then again, I didn't want to touch one, for fear of being cruel. But the odds didn't seem high that I would expose anyone, embarrass anyone. I thought again of the intact wrapping, as the boy smiled and put out his tongue. Four or five flecks of metal shone, the bits he hadn't managed to devour, along with a few drippings of spit-diluted blood from minor cuts to his mouth. Whatever was scraping down his passageways, along his inner linings, seemed keen enough to shred them.

The apprentices set a bowl filled with sacred brown water on the checkered mat. They passed a cigarette among them, smoking it carefully until the ash dangled. A young man took the ash in his hands, rubbed his palms, submerged his hands in the water, continuing to rub. When he pulled his hands up, he dropped a rolled 5,000 leone bill on the mat. Like the other apprentices, he wore no shirt; he could have no trick pouches or sleeves. The bill was perfectly dry.

They spread the secretly blessed liquid over their bodies, and held a flaming stick, burned almost to coal, against their skin. They pressed it long. They suggested I dip my hand in the bowl.

Fire sprung from my palm. I jerked my hand from the stick. They laughed. "Leave it," I heard Michael's voice behind me in the dark.

"Are you sure about this?"

"I am sure."

I forced myself. The flames rippled and leaned, dancing, and the wood glowed. My flesh started to prickle and sting. Whatever power might be in the water was beginning to wear off, or wasn't fully applicable to me. "Okay, okay," I said. They asked if I wanted to take off my shirt and try the liquid and then the fire on my body, as they had done. I declined.

They asked again, for me to do as they had done, after a young man had reslathered his chest and belly, lain down on his back, set a rice mortar filled with dirt on his front, and let the others pound away with a thick, five-foot-long pestle. They beckoned me to pound, too, so I wouldn't think they were holding back. The pestle was heavy, and after two or three blows at half strength, I brought the weight down with everything I had. The apprentice beneath me was silent, unfazed. His ribs scarcely gave. I went on with my thrusts, harder. Everyone laughed. "You are going to exhaust yourself," Michael said, pitying. The recumbent apprentice smiled. The dirt in the mortar must absorb the energy of the blows, I thought to myself. But when they invited me to lie down, I declined again.

The demonstration ended with the turning of cassava into sugar. The root was diced into a small amount of the special murky liquid. An apprentice let himself be searched, the pockets of his shorts flipped inside out, before he sat down. A brown blanket was displayed, ordinary on both sides. It was draped over him, covering him completely. A minute passed, the blanket un-moving. When the apprentice emerged, he offered me a large bowl full of white grains.

"He would like you to taste it," Michael said.

I dabbed cautiously with one finger. I don't know what harm I expected to come.

"Is it sweet?"

I confirmed that it was.

And yes, I understood that the apprentice had almost surely executed some trick under the blanket. Yet there seemed no way he could have done it, nowhere such a quantity of sugar could have been hidden. Had it been buried in the ground? Had he somehow managed to dig it out, despite the mat and never disturbing the blanket? But even if it had been a hoax, did it matter? Here, in Gebau's dirt yard in the middle of the lowest nation on earth, something baffling, something entrancing and even bedazzling in its unceremonial way, had been created from next to nothing. What is magic if not that?

From such power Michael believed that he would offer new medicine to the world, that he would beckon a multitude to this land. All would be united, all prospering, all healed.

"That is my dream."

Acknowledgments

Though this book tells the stories of only a few, it is built on talks with hundreds. For their generosity, patience, and candor, I am indebted to everyone in Sierra Leone who, despite the most difficult circumstances, taught me what I needed to learn and led me where I needed to go. My gratitude to those I wrote about—those who allowed me so often into their lives—is beyond measure. Among those in the background, F. A. Boima and Paul Moseray gave powerful insight. And Aya Shneerson, in Sierra Leone and before that in southern Sudan, pointed always in the right direction.

For delicate direction and keen support of my writing, I am endlessly thankful to my editor, John Glusman, and to Aodaoin O'Floinn, Jeff Seroy, Ellen Browning, Kim Hilario, and everyone at Farrar, Straus and Giroux. Special thanks to my paperback editor, Amber Qureshi, at Picador. For faith in my far-flung ideas, I am much more than lucky to have Suzanne Gluck as my agent; my immense gratitude goes to her, as ever, and to Karen Gerwin, Emily Nurkin, Eugenie Furniss, Tracy Fisher, and all at William Morris.

Many thanks to Tina Brown and Tom Watson at *Talk* and Lewis Lapham and Colin Harrison at *Harper's*, who first sent me to report on Africa; to Bill Hogeland and Roland Kelts, who were invaluable readers, willing always to debate the implications and inflection of a sentence; and to Peter Hedges, whose few words of advice allowed me to find my own words.

I would scarcely have known of Sierra Leone were it not for the daily journalists who covered the country's civil war and who were far more brave than I in their pursuit of stories that the world, in general, never read, heard, watched. Some of those journalists, Sierra Leonean and expatriate, were killed as they worked or in reprisal for their reporting. They are: Alpha Amadu Bah, Jenner Cole, Saoman Conteh, Abdulai Jumah Jalloh, Ishmael Jalloh, Mabay Kamara, Paul Mansaray, Miguel Gil Moreno de Mora, James Ogogo, Kurt Schork, Edward Smith, Myles Tierney, and Munir Tiray. My debt to them is inexpressible and, in a sense, unspeakable.

Between my trips to Sierra Leone, I kept up with events there through the news-compilations of Peter Andersen on his Sierra Leone Web. I relied as well on the dispatches of the BBC and the reports of Human Rights Watch.

For understanding of Sierra Leone's history, politics, and culture, I drew from works by Arthur Abraham, Michael Craton, Philip Curtin, Basil Davidson, Christopher Fyfe, C. Magbaily Fyle, John Hargreaves, John L. Hirsch, John Iliffe, Michael Jackson, Lawrence James, Milan Kalous, Alexander Kup, E.C.P. Lascelles, Thomas Pakenham, John Reader, Paul Richards, A.B.C. Sibthorpe, A. K. Turay, Francis Utting, C. Braithwaite Wallis, and Richard West. *Africana: The Encyclopedia of the African and African American Experience*, edited by Kwame Anthony Appiah and Henry Louis Gates, Jr., was a source of important perspective. Throughout my research, the library of the Shomburg Center for Research in Black Culture was essential.

Essential in so many ways were the love and memory of my mother, Marilyn Bergner; the love and help of my mother-in-law, Jean Northup; and the love and support and belief of my father, Lawrence Bergner. And without the love of my wife, Nancy Northup, and my children, Natalie and Miles, all would have been impossible.